THE INSIDER'S GUIDE TO
THE BEST SKIING
COLORADO

Other Books by Lito Tejada-Flores:

WILDERNESS SKIING
WILDWATER
  The Sierra Club Guide to Kayaking and Whitewater Boating
BACKCOUNTRY SKIING
  The Sierra Club Guide to Skiing off the Beaten Track
BREAKTHROUGH ON SKIS
  How to Get Out of the Intermediate Rut

Other Guides in this series:

THE INSIDER'S GUIDE TO THE BEST SKIING IN UTAH
  by Peter Shelton

THE INSIDER'S GUIDE TO
THE BEST SKIING
COLORADO

NEWLY REVISED

BY LITO TEJADA-FLORES

WESTERN EYE PRESS

TELLURIDE

THE INSIDER'S GUIDE
TO THE BEST SKIING
IN COLORADO
second edition
Western Eye Press
Box 917, Telluride Colorado 81435

© 1988 by Lito Tejada-Flores

ISBN 0-941283-04-6
This book was written, illustrated,
designed and typeset by the author
on a Macintosh computer and laid-out
for printing with Aldus PageMaker.
The ski trail-map sketches
were created with Illustrator 88
and a Datacopy scanner loaned by
Peter Spencer of Spencer Technology.

All photos © 1988 by Linde Waidhofer,
(cover skier, Tom Stillo)

Printed in Ann Arbor, Michigan
by Malloy Lithographing, Inc.

Western Eye Press is a small
Colorado-based publishing adventure
dedicated to publishing handsome,
works on the Rockies and the West,
and books by western authors.
Our other titles to date include
the photo-art book, *HIGH COLOR*,
Spectacular Wildflowers of the Rockies,
by Linde Waidhofer;
YELLOWSTONE TO YOSEMITE,
Early Adventures in the Mountain West,
illustrated by Thomas Moran; and
the second volume in this series,
The Insider's Guide to the Best Skiing in Utah.

Special thanks to many friends at
different Colorado ski areas who
read individual chapters and made
so many valuable suggestions. In that
sense this book is the work of many
"insiders," not just one.

CONTENTS

INTRODUCTION

I wrote the first version of this guidebook with one question looming large: Would this book really be as useful as I hoped? The answer apparently was yes, since the first edition sold out in one season. A perfect opportunity, I thought, to revise it and update it. And that's what you're looking at now. A new volume that's been buffed, polished, and fine-tuned, that contains new information on new lifts, new runs, and new treats for Colorado skiers and visitors....

THE INSIDER'S VIEW

Welcome to a new kind of skier's guide— I'm promising you a special view of Colorado skiing, an insider's perspective. What does that mean? The ideal insider is someone who lives at a ski resort, who has spent years ferreting out its secrets and who's willing, even eager to share them. Someone who sets his alarm for 5 a.m. to be the first skier in line on a powder morning; and who still knows where to find the last untracked stash, two days after a storm. Someone who can find the warmest, sunniest run on the coldest day of winter, the best shaped moguls, the most interesting groomed runs. Someone who knows the best boot fitter, or the best ski tuner in town, and wants to tell you about them.... The insider.

It's a tall order to give you the inside scoop on the sixteen major ski areas and resorts in Colorado. Sure, I've lived at some, taught skiing at others, and visited others so often they feel like home. But I can't claim total, intimate, in-depth knowledge of all of them – although I've certainly skied all of them. So what I'm offering in this guide is a multiple look at things. My own impressions, naturally, a very personal, very opinionated view. But I've also gone out of my way to round up and consult local insiders in virtually all these resorts. To ask them for the sort of information I could only know about my own mountain. And then too, I've looked at all these Colorado ski areas from my ski instructor's point of view. Which is a very special sort of insider's perspective.

When an experienced ski instructor starts teaching on a new mountain, the first task is to figure out all the basic sorts of information that I want to share with you in this book: Which are the best ways down in the evenings? The best runs to warm up on in the morning? Where are the traffic bottlenecks and how to avoid them? How to find the best ski lunch without wasting any time or standing in line? Above all, what slopes offer just the right blend of challenge and comfort for each student – that is to say, for each level of skier?

It's a real art to figure all this out in a day or two, in order to give your students the absolute best experience possible. But that's what good ski instructors do, what I've done for years, what I've tried to do for you in this book.

My insider's perspective is definitely that of a ski instructor. The kind of experienced, enthusiastic, conscientious instructor who makes sure that no one ever has a bad time on his or her mountain. Ski teaching has been a twenty-year passion for me, one of the most rewarding things I've ever done. Two years ago, I put this passion – all the lessons I've taught and all the lessons I've learned – into a book, *Breakthrough on Skis, How to Get Out of the Intermediate Rut.* This was one way of sharing an insider's perspective. So it's natural that my goals in writing this guide should also include helping you ski better.

It doesn't seem fair to say: "Since you're only a certain level of skier you'll only enjoy such and such a slope," when I also believe that you can make dramatic progress and enjoy harder slopes too. I've yielded to this optimism and included a series of short instructional tips. They're found at the end of chapters on different ski areas in such a way that the ski techniques covered relate to the special conditions of each area. These Ski Tech sections, are necessarily brief, shorthand compressed tips to help you cope with some of the special challenges, or charms, of Colorado skiing as exemplified by the sixteen ski areas in this guide.

You'll discover that this is, first and foremost, a book about *skiing.* This is not a book cramed full of statistics, lists, addresses, prices, shopping and lodging tips. This is a book full of experiences to share, a book full of skiing, great skiing – the best skiing in Colorado.

WHY COLORADO?

Why ski Colorado? It's not a dumb question. There are a host of reasons – all far more persuasive than George Leigh Mallory's reason for climbing Everest: "Because it's there."

For starters, Rocky Mountain skiing, and that means Colorado skiing, is different from anything one can find in the Far West, the Pacific Northwest or the East. Not because they attach lift tickets differently out here, or ski with a different technique or equipment, but because the snow is so different. Snow is lighter and drier throughout the entire Rocky Mountain region than anywhere else in the country. And while Colorado can't really dispute Utah's claim to the lightest, driest snow of all, there is still more of it – more light snow, and more modern ski areas to render it accessible – in Colorado than anywhere else.

Why is the snow out here so light, so dry, so fine? It's because the Rockies enjoy (and occasionally suffer from) an altogether different climate – a so-called "continental" rather than a "maritime" climate. All other ski regions in the U.S. are close to coasts, to oceans. And water means wet; wet sand at the beach, wet snow at Tahoe, or at Sugarbush Vermont, or at White Pass Washington. But when storms travel a thousand miles or so, over intervening ranges and rain-shadowed desert basins, losing moisture all the way, what they finally drop on mountain ranges in the center of the continent is light dry fluff. The name's the same (only Eskimos, we're told, have over twenty separate words for different types of snow) and so is the color, white on white on white, but there the similarity ends. Rocky Mountain snow, Colorado snow, is drier, lighter, fluffier than I can possibly tell you in words, than you can possibly imagine if you haven't already skied there.

Why is light snow important? Light, dry "continental" snow versus wetter, heavier "maritime" snow? Simple: you ski better, much better, on light, dry snow. That's a promise. You'll ski better in Colorado than you do at home (unless this is home). There. The cat's out of the bag. This is the real reason skiers from all over tend to get hooked on Rocky Mountain skiing and return, year after year after year. This promise – that you'll actually ski better – is not clearly articulated on the cover of any of the hundreds of thousands of ski/tourist brochures that tout the virtues of the Colorado ski experience. But an enormous segment of the tourist economy of the state depends on this particular promise being legitimate. It is. I've never met a skier yet (myself included) that didn't fall for this delicious ego-stroking snow. You will too. No matter what your current favorite ski area, you'll eventually be tempted by the Colorado. And you'll eventually become hooked. Perfect snow is a strong drug.

That's not all. The resort flavor of Colorado skiing is unlike anything you can find elsewhere. One could say that what distinguishes Colorado from other parts of the country is not the number of great ski areas, but the number of great ski resorts . I'm not splitting hairs. A ski area is a mountain equipped for skiing, period. While a ski resort offers far more than just skiing – life at the bottom of the mountain must be as intriguing, as intoxicating, as turns on the hill. A real ski resort has got to offer more than strip development, motel-style or minimalist condo accommodation, and endless parking lots. The majority of Colorado ski areas are real "resorts" in this sense. The very best ski resorts of all are actually entire villages or towns – communities where the whole rhythm and fabric of life, the atmosphere in the streets, the focus and passion of locals as well as visitors, is inextricably tied to skiing. Great ski villages are easy to find in the Alps, all too rare in the States, and most of those we have are in Colorado.

There are a lot of true ski villages here. But I've promised you a tour of the *best skiing* in Colorado, not just the best resorts, so we'll also be visiting a couple of areas that don't qualify as proper resorts but do offer dynamite skiing. Still I've been very choosy. There are more than thirty ski areas in the state. In this book we're going to visit only sixteen. The sixteen best. But while it's easy to talk about Colorado's "best skiing" in a general way, I would be hard pressed to vote for Colorado's best single resort.

I live in one Colorado ski town, Telluride – a place I fell in love with thirteen years ago and still adore, but which I wouldn't dare claim was "the best." Every good ski resort is somebody's favorite. The special quality of light, of snow, of friends you're skiing with, of your own state of mind and body – all this makes one day, one place, one memory the best. With any luck you'll have numerous "best days" on Colorado slopes. So I'll leave ultimate judgments to each reader.

But there is still a pecking order. If Colorado can be called the capital of American skiing, then it must be said that the twin capitals of Colorado skiing are Vail and Aspen. And this is where we'll start our insider's tour: with these two ski towns that set the standards by which others resorts are judged. Two leaders in a wave of change that is altering the nature and quality of Colorado skiing.

THE WHITE REVOLUTION

Colorado is ski country par excellence . Medium sized ski resorts in Colorado would be giants in other states; giants here are in a class by themselves. There are so many skiers now in Colorado, both locals and out-of-state vacationers, and the competition between resorts to attract

these skiers is so fierce, that the average level of skier service and
amenities – what you get for your skiing dollar – is now higher here than
anywhere in the country. Even more important you're getting something
new for that dollar.

For generations, lift lines have been the bane of downhill skiers'
existence. Lift lines haven't disappeared in Colorado but they're on the
way out. The solution, like the problem itself comes from technology.
New lifts with higher capacity and dramatically faster uphill speeds are
not only eliminating lift lines, but cutting the total time you spend going
uphill almost in half. The cunning machines responsible for this white
revolution are high-speed, detachable four-person chairlifts, also known
as express lifts or super chairs. They work just like gondolas, moving at
very slow speeds through the loading and unloading stations, then
sliding down a ramp to gather speed and hook on to a fast moving cable.
By now, all American skiers have heard of detachable quad chairs, and
most have ridden them, if only occasionally. But the super price tag for
these super lifts (well over a million dollars each) means that you're not
likely to see them at small weekend ski areas. The revolution didn't
start in earnest until Vail decided to install four high-speed quads in the
summer of '85 (although the first detachable quad in Colorado had ben
built at Breckenridge years earlier). In one season, the skiing and traffic
patterns on Vail mountain were totally transformed. And what the
Denver press quickly dubbed "The Quad Wars" were unleashed between
major Colorado ski areas, each looking to be more up-to-date than the
next. The winners, obviously, were Colorado skiers.

While it's true that lift prices have risen here in recent years largely
as a result of these new lifts – and sometimes risen dramatically – the
cost of quality skiing has come down just as dramatically. It's come
down, that is, if you think in terms of dollars per vertical feet. It's a
brave new world out there. Skiers who never ever managed to get
enough runs in one day are now quitting at 2:30 in the afternoon because
they've skied so much, so fast, their legs are starting to complain. A
nice feeling actually.

The radical revamping of lift infrastructure is only the most obvious
change in the Colorado ski scene. On closer inspection, the new lifts are
just part of a generalized upgrading of mountain facilities. Some areas
have greatly extended their snowmaking – already nearly universal as a
form of pre-Christmas, early-season insurance. Many areas have
completely remodeled their base facilities and on-mountain eateries in
recent years. On-mountain, sit-down restaurants are proliferating as
alternatives to the usual dreadful cafeteria fare. All told, Colorado ski

corporations have just lived through a cycle of investment in the future of a magnitude never before seen. And in the base villages below the lifts, skier services have become more sophisticated than ever. Like I said, it's a white revolution.

A new form of "skiing" has appeared as well. I mean snowboarding, a controversial rarity a few years ago, now pretty common at most Colorado resorts. Snowboarding is challenging and graceful, but above all it's new. Which is exactly why it's so attractive to younger kids and teenagers who, on the slopes as in everyday life, delight in anything that sets them apart from their parents' generation. Far from being a subversive threat to the integrity of our sport, as some over-reacting ski area managers initially perceived it to be, snowboarding has actually brought more families to the slopes together; has given more kids a reason to accompany their parents willingly rather than grudgingly on annual Colorado ski jaunts. Irrationally, a few areas are still holding out against this latest import to the slopes (originally an American idea, snowboarding was enthusiastically embraced and developed in the Alps before returning to our shores). In recent seasons, most Colorado ski areas have relented and welcomed snowboarders as just one more facet of the white revolution; the remaining hold-out areas will be shamed into it soon.

The white revolution in Colorado skiing is what first led me to write this book. Super lifts have changed more than just uphill access times. They've changed the way to think about these Colorado mountains, the way to ski them, the way to plan your day for maximum enjoyment. And that's what this book is about....

Enough introductions. We've got a lot of resorts to visit, a lot of glorious white miles to cover together. Needless to say, doing the "research" for this guide – skiing all these Colorado areas in the course of one winter, and re-skiing them often since in search of "revisions" and new hot tips – was fantastic. A ski-writer's fantasy. I hope you'll share this fantasy with me. I know it's waiting for you on Colorado ski slopes.

NOTE: Throughout this book I'll often describe runs as green, blue or black. This is a reference to our national trail rating system in which green circles mean "easiest," blue squares "more difficult" and black diamonds "most difficult." Areas sometimes add a double black diamond designation meaning "experts only." Trouble is, the same color may not mean the same thing on different mountains. Where this is the case, I'll tip you off that the area in question tends to over-grade or under-grade its runs.

PART I

THE VAIL VALLEY

CHAPTER 1   VAIL

In my introduction I claim that Vail and Aspen are the twin capitals, not only of Colorado skiing, but of American skiing. This said, I should underline the differences between them: Aspen is older and richer in history and community, but its skiing is much more diffuse, fragmented and spread out across four separate mountains. While Vail – well, Vail is a newer and brasher resort, but Vail has it all, all together, all at once. Vail is the most complete all-around ski mountain and seamlessly polished resort/vacation machine you can imagine. It's probably the easiest place I know where a skier, any skier, can have a perfect day, any day.

It's no accident that Vail is the first ski resort we're visiting in this guide. Or that Vail comes in first by most terms with which the ski world measures success: number of visitors, size of ski school, the sheer boggling sums that vacationing skiers leave in this small jewel of a ski-resort town, and above all in the size of it's skiable terrain. It's big, really big, And, as if to render the term "big" even harder to grasp, Vail has recently *doubled* its total skiable acreage by opening five new "Back Bowls" for the 88/89 season. Vail today has more skiable acreage than all four major ski areas in nearby Summit County – Keystone, Arapahoe, Breckenridge and Copper Mountain – put together. The 1989 season also marked a new high point in the international recognition of this Colorado classic, the hosting of the FIS World Championships in the Vail Valley.

But Vail is no zoo. Both town and mountain "work" in ways that other ski areas only dream about. Vail Village is the only true pedestrian ski town in America – a lesson that resort planners everywhere should have learned from, and generally haven't.

Virtually every one of the fifteen major Colorado ski areas we visit in this *Insider's Guide* can boast one or two special facets of the skiing experience at which it absolutely excels: the grandest views, the best beginner area, the finest glades. Vail too; it's multiple Back Bowls are easily the best "powder preserve" in the state. But – an important but – no other American resort offers as complete a spectrum of ski options, on one mountain, for every level skier. A family group spanning three generations and twice that many skiing styles and ability levels can ski Vail mountain, meet for lunch, separate and meet again in the evening with no frustrations. Each individual, like the proverbial blind men describing an elephant, will be skiing his or her own version of Vail mountain. This kind of an all-around ski mountain, where no one need be bored, frustrated or overchallenged, is a rarity.

In addition, Vail is probably the most ego-building ski mountain I know. For a curious reason: Vail's first trails and runs were cut by early-day ski fanatics, graduates of the 10th mountain division, armed only with chain saws and visions of wide-open skiing they'd enjoyed in the Alps after World War II. Unencumbered by university degrees in ski area design, computer-generated mountain models and environmental impact statements, they just went and cut themselves exceptionally wide runs. Wide runs have a subconscious but critical effect on a skier's frame of mind: with no potential obstacles looming up on either side, all skiers ski better. Vail's runs are wider and thus, in a purely artificial way, more "natural" than what most skiers are used to. A liberating experience.

Enough generalizations. Let's look at this beauty of a ski mountain in detail:

THE MULTIPLE WORLDS OF VAIL MOUNTAIN

Looking up from the village one can easily underestimate Vail mountain. Sure it's big, or more accurately wide, very wide, but all you can see from below is a friendly forest cut here and there by white ribbon runs, rising gently, then sloping back out of sight. Most of the mountain, in fact, is out of sight. From Vail Village the original town center, you catch a couple of tantalizing glimpses of steep ridge runs high up. From Lionshead, the second resort center to the west, the upper mountain is totally invisible. But it's up there, waiting.

Vail is a wide mountain, not a tall or narrow one, defined by a long ridge running roughly east west. The whole ski area measures over 7 miles across, east to west. It's also a two-faced ski mountain, not merely in the sense of facing both north and south, but of exhibiting a totally different character on each side. Both faces, luckily, are lovable. Dropping down toward the twin centers of Vail Village and Lionshead, the front or north face is classic Colorado ski country: dark green mountainsides of dense forest that only ingenuity and chain saws could have transformed into a big ski area. (Colorado I should explain has a remarkably high tree line compared to most other mountain regions in America, with evergreen forest growing right up to 12,000 feet.) The front side offers mostly trail skiing with only a few wide-open clearings and small bowls high up.

The back side of Vail mountain is another story. Forest fires in the late 19th century stripped the slopes of timber, and the intense solar radiation and evaporation on these high south-facing slopes kept the forest from ever reestablishing itself. Hence the Back Bowls, Vail's not-so-secret advantage. Not one back bowl, but a whole series, one after the other, mile after mile.

From Vail's opening in 1962 until 1988, only two of these bowls, *Sun Down* and *Sun Up*, were part of the ski area, and they literally made Vail's reputation as a ski area. These two bowls are, in fact, huge. But they've been dwarfed in area, if not in reputation, by the four new bowls, *China, Teacup, Siberia* and *Mongolia Bowls*, opened up to skiers by a major expansion project in the summer of '88. The good news for most Vail fans is that these new bowls are somewhat easier-angled, hence more accessible to average skiers, than *Sun Down* and *Sun Up*. The new bowls are definitely not experts-only terrain, but they're just as imposing, as empty and white, just as breathtaking as the two classic bowls.

Vail mountain is large enough that skiers often spend whole days skiing only one part of it, without running out of new runs to try. To those who know it well, Vail mountain seems like a collection of separate but contiguous ski areas, each with it's own feeling and character, its own style of skiing:

Organize your mental map of Vail mountain into nine different zones. On the front side, from east to west: Lionshead, the Middle Mountain, Mid-Vail, the Northeast, the Far East and Golden Peak; then comes Game Creek, a bowl in a side valley that's neither on the front nor back side of the mountain; and finally, on the backside, the Classic Bowls, and the New Bowls. Each is the equivalent of a smaller ski area in its own right. To start, I'm going to paint a thumbnail sketch of each of these zones, then we'll visit them in more detail as I discuss Vail for different levels of skiers.

Lionshead skiing, at the extreme western side of Vail Mountain, is a labyrinth of long sinuous runs, cleanly separated paths through elegant forests of lodgepole and spruce. There isn't a lot of steep or difficult skiing in this area, but there is a lot of good relaxed cruising, and often a pleasing feeling of solitude as the runs are visually cut off from one another.

The Middle Mountain is a nebulous zone, that is somewhat under-skied, underappreciated. I'm talking about the runs dropping below *Eagle's Nest Ridge* from *Avanti* across to *Columbine*; and their lower extensions, dropping all the way down into Vail Village. Because it doesn't have a real name, a unique geographical identity or mystique, this center region of the front face is skied less than it deserves; usually only as a way home at the end of the day. But World Cup GS and downhill races are held on this middle mountain. These are very long, very interesting runs. Don't forget them. A new detachable lift, the Avanti Express, which replaces two fixed grip chairs (2 and 17) on the Middle Mountain, makes skiing this zone a more enjoyable and more "modern" experience. It also speeds up the crossing time from one side of the mountain to the other.

Mid-Vail, of course, is the classic mid-mountain restaurant, remod-eled endlessly into today's giant hub. But I also use the name for the wide basins above this restaurant. This Mid-Vail area is not quite a "bowl" in the pure sense, but two open alpine valleys, served by two lifts, a quad and a triple, and chock full of runs – a great variety of runs that are interesting but short and usually a trifle crowded. I'm not sure if crowded is the right word, but if any zone on Vail mountain seems crowded this is it. Why? Because the fanciest lift out of Vail Village, the Vista Bahn quad, arrives smack at Mid-Vail with an endless stream of skiers and, through some sort of gregarious herd instinct, many tend to just stay right there. Don't fall into this trap. Mid-Vail skiing is like a visit to a lovely but small ski area within a giant ski area; if you spend all day on the slopes above Mid-Vail you will be enjoying only a frac-tion of what Vail has to offer.

From Mid-Vail itself, chair 4 carries skiers up to the top of Vail mountain. Calling it a summit would give too much dignity to what is little more than the highest bump on a system of ridgelines, but it's still the top. Locals call it "PHQ" for Patrol Headquarters. PHQ is also the key crossroads on the mountain where lift 5 comes out of the Classic Bowls, and lift 11 arrives from the Northeast side.

The Northeast side of Vail lies just around the corner, east of the

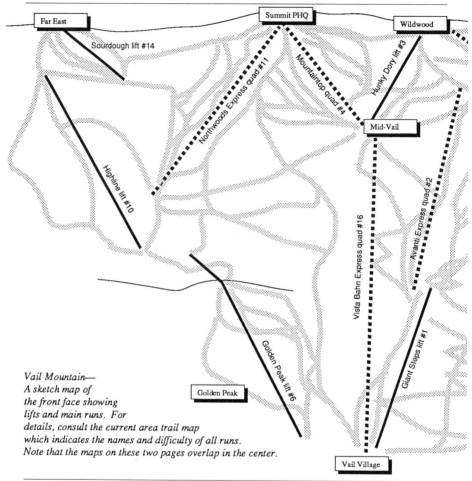

Vail Mountain—
A sketch map of
the front face showing
lifts and main runs. For
details, consult the current area trail map
which indicates the names and difficulty of all runs.
Note that the maps on these two pages overlap in the center.

Mid-Vail basin. This is an area of steep forests, lots of steep runs, lots
of hard skiing. In fact, the most challenging skiing in Vail, if not the
most beautiful, and the greatest concentration of black runs on the front
side, is all to be found over here in the Northeast. There are rolling
swooping "easy" black trails, there are steep and moguled ridgelines,
there is even a kind of bump skiers' ghetto, chair 10 with its demanding
Double Blacks. The Northeast is where serious Vail skiers head, at least
once a day, for a real workout.

Far East is a small area at the east end of the upper mountain, a
long, long way from where we began in Lionshead. There's only one
lift up here, chair 14, a triple. This is a novice skiers' paradise of gentle,
friendly, low-angle runs where inexperienced skiers can cut loose, and

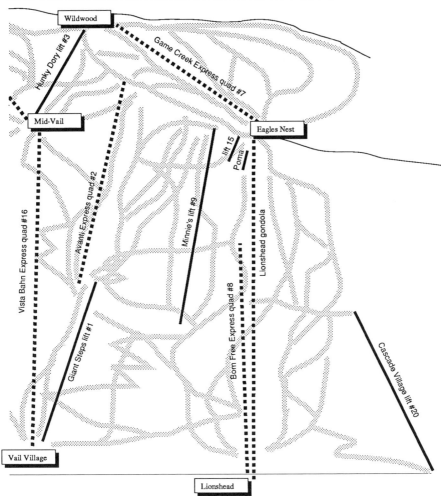

soon transcend their novice limits. It has now acquired a new importance as the the gateway to the New Bowls. The Far East can be reached
by taking lifts 6 and 10 to 14, but it's often faster to take the Vista Bahn
and lift 4, then cut across to lift 14 on *Timberline Catwalk.*

Golden Peak is also at the far eastern end of Vail mountain, but low
down, right out of the village. It's actually a separate sub-peak or
detached ridge, named for the fiery autumn colors in its dense aspen
stands. Golden Peak has one long double chair (lift 6), a small beginners' chair (lift 12) and teaching area. It feels, and is, somewhat cut off
from the rest of the mountain. While there are a few comfortable
intermediate runs down here, Golden Peak is primarily a ski-racing and
race-training enclave and children's skiing area.

And then there are the bowls. Vail simply wouldn't be Vail without these white spots on the map, in skier's minds, these empty delicious open arenas of white on white.

Game Creek Bowl lies over the ridge from Mid-Vail, via lift 3. Game Creek used to be a smaller place altogether, but with the cutting of a number of new runs on its left or north-facing flank and the upgrading of chair 7 to full detachable status, Game Creek has become one of the most complete intermediate ski zones on the mountain.

The Classic Bowls and the *New Bowls*, are the frosting on Vail's cake and we'll visit them in more detail in the next sections. But to complete your mental map, your birds-eye overview, remember that the two Classic Bowls, *Sun Down* and *Sun Up*, lie just behind PHQ. You dive into them from the top of the mountain and come back out to PHQ via lift 5. Although you can also enter *Sun Down* from the top of chairs 3 and 7, and even sneak into the far side of *Sun Up* from chair 14. The five New Bowls are strung like pearls along Vail's main ridge, to the east of the Classic Bowls and together they boast a skiing acreage equal to the rest of Vail Mountain. As we'll see, the New Bowls have truly changed the feel and flavor of Vail skiing. They are most easily entered from chair 14 and the Far East, but can be reached from PHQ via *Sleepytime* catwalk. From west to east, you'll encounter *Tea Cup Bowl, China Bowl, Siberia Bowl* and *Inner* and *Outer Mongolia Bowls*. They are served by a quad lift, the Orient Express, and a short surface lift.

And that's Vail, a totally diverse mountain, a world of sub-worlds, the biggest of the big ones. The common denominator at Vail mountain is its user-friendly character. Most runs lie square in the fall line, most steeps offer a way around for skiers who suddenly realize they don't belong there, and most runs are steady and continuous. Vail is perhaps more of a cruiser's mountain than an adventure mountain. But Vail cruising is sensational, and there are still enough challenges on this monster to keep hyperactive hot shots happy for a long time. Let's get more specific. I want to tell you about my favorite runs, the best runs for different level skiers.

VAIL FOR GOOD SKIERS

The term "good skiers" sounds pretty vague, but I have real skiers in mind: Skiers who feel at home on their skis, who have probably been skiing for quite a few seasons, who spend most of their time on blue slopes and look pretty spiffy on moderate terrain. Skiers who can definitely get down a black slope, or two, or three, but don't hang out all day on these steep, moguled runs. Skiers who can cope with fresh snow and powder but who don't exactly dance through it. Skiers who ski the whole mountain but don't yet "own" it, who don't make heads turn with admiration as they flash by. But who flash by nonetheless, and enjoy skiing at a pretty good clip when the slopes are comfortable. Sound like you? You're in luck. Vail is a paradise, a Valhalla for good skiers.

This is exactly the sort of skier that the Mid-Vail runs are designed for. But as I've already said, although popular, Mid-Vail is both limited and limiting if you ski there too much. The finest run here is *Cappuccino*. The relatively obscure and narrow entrance from *Swingsville Ridge* hides a real gem. *Cappuccino* is more varied in pitch than the runs on either side and there are wonderful stands of widely spaced trees that invite you into a kind of natural giant-slalom game. The widest run in this area is *Ramshorn*, which is marked green but is actually indistinguishable from a lot of the blue runs around it. (Someone apparently felt the need to to show green runs on the map from the top of the mountain down to Mid-Vail, which is why *Ramshorn*, *Swingsville* and *Christmas* are colored green in defiance of common sense.) For me, the extra space on *Ramshorn* is a real incentive to fast big turns. You can indulge in a few extra miles per hour here without bugging (or even coming close to) other skiers.

After warming up with a couple of runs on the slopes above Mid-Vail, I recommend a couple of early-morning cruisers down *Northwoods* and *Northstar*. The charm of *Northwoods* is its length and the fact that you are skiing down continuously changing mountain shapes: rolls, dips, short flats and inviting drops. *Northstar*, which is half-hidden in the forest to the left of *Northwoods*, is the same sort of run only more so: the steeps somewhat steeper, the rolls and drop-aways more inviting. Although marked black on the trail map, *Northstar* isn't really very hard; but unlike *Northwoods* there are no ways around the steeper pitches. Return to the top is rapid via chair 11, the Northwoods Express quad, which can also brings you back from *Riva Ridge*, another "easy" black slope, providing you turn right onto *Trans Montane Catwalk* at the bottom of the actual ridge of *Riva Ridge*. Before this handy catwalk leading back to chair 11 was cut, *Riva Ridge* used to be reserved only for skiing home at the end of the day, or skiing down to the village for lunch. Now skiers can also take advantage of the high-speed return offered by the Vista Bahn and chair 4 to ski full moutain runs here: Riva to Tourist Trap to the Village via Mill Creek.

Another paradise for good skiers is *Game Creek Bowl*, where the black runs feel almost bluish (i.e. friendly) and the blue runs are continuous enough to feel blue-black (i.e. dramatic if not difficult). Lift 7, a high-speed quad, keeps you circulating at a brisk clip. My favorite run here is *Dealer's Choice*, a masterpiece of trail cutting. The runs on the right side of *Game Creek Bowl* (looking down) are all marked black; but they are short and very wide, offering good skiers lots of options, rather than only one or two forced paths through bumpy obstacles as black slopes so often do. These runs, *Deuces Wild*, *Faro* and *Ouzo* are almost treeless, which makes them into friendly, non-threatening powder lines after a storm. A good place to practice and develop your deep-snow skills.

How about the Back Bowls for "good skiers"? Why not? But please, not every slope, not every run back there. Until the opening of Vail's New Bowls for the 88/89 season your choices in the back were much more limited. In fact, the New Bowls are generally much less steep, hence more inviting to average skiers than *Sun Down* and *Sun Up Bowls* ever were. So start out in *China Bowl*.

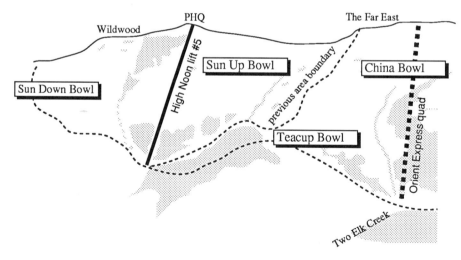

Vail's Back Bowls—
the largest most beautiful open-bowl ski terrain in Colorado—
a sketch map showing lifts and large-scale skiing zones:
On this page: Vail's two Classic Bowls. These bowls which used to appear immense,
are now only a small part of the total Back-Bowl experience.
See the current trail maps for details.

What's it like back here aside from big? The New Bowls are so vast that you can actually find almost every kind of skiing there, but the eastern sides of of both *China* and *Siberia Bowls* (on your left looking down) are wide and fairly low-angle slopes. Ideal terrain for your first Back Bowl adventures. In addition, Vail manages to keep the two main routes into *China Bowl* groomed; these are upper *Poppy Fields* and the gentler east side of *Dragon's Teeth*. And despite the black-only trail designation on the map, they're a breeze. In next-door *Siberia Bowl*, the easiest skiing is also found on the west-facing flank, long known to the patrol as the *Bolshoi Ballroom*; and down the large central area, *Gorky Park*. These are stress-free runs, Back Bowls skiing for everyone.

On the east side of *China Bowl* you'll find *Shangrila*, an area of sparse trees that offers skiers multiple glade-like paths, none of which are hard. You can ski run after run here, and never dive through the same grove of trees twice. These *Shangrila* trees are an important exception in the middle of this wide-open treeless terrain, for they allow (even encourage) Back-Bowl skiing on stormy days by providing extra visibility and shelter from wind.

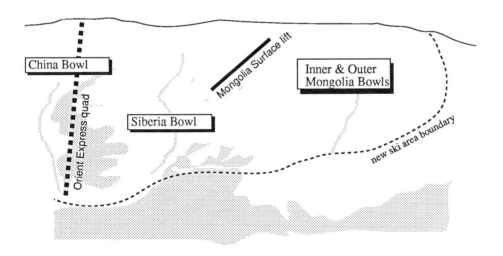

Vail's New Bowls—
a sketch map showing the expansion of Vail's Back Bowl terrain. On this page, the New Bowls.
(Note that these two sketches overlap in the center.) Check the ski area trail map for details and
for the names of the many newly christened runs and sub-zones in this vast space.

The western sides (on your right looking down) of these two big bowls, *China* and *Siberia*, are fairly steep and for the most part, should be considered legitimate, black, expert terrain. They also receive a good deal more wind-blown snow than do the Classic Bowls, so that when the patrol records 6 or 7 inches of new snow at PHQ, lines like *Jade Glade, Bamboo Chute*, and the *Genghis Kahn* wall on the west side of China Bowl can be filled in with 18 to 24 inches. Not bad! I owe you one more caveat here: *Rasputin's Revenge*, the steep face directly beneath the western ridge of *Siberia Bowl*, is also a classic Back Bowl powder shot, but it's the single steepest pitch in the Back—leave it for experts.

Teacup Bowl, at the lower west end of the New Bowls is also special case. It's likely to be best in springtime, corn-snow conditions, and isn't steep enough for classic powder skiing. At the eastern end of the New Bowls, *Inner and OuterMongolia Bowls*, (know to locals as *"Innie"* and *"Outie"*) are big and friendly but perhaps a bit too low-angle to attract a lot of skiers. They are also a bit out of the main traffic pattern here, as you must reach them by traversing across *Siberia Bowl* and then taking the Mongolia platter lift. The further east you go in Mongolia Bowl the gentler the terrain. It's destined to become a mecca for telemark skiers on their more delicate three-pin Nordic gear.

It must be said that the New Bowls have already had a terrific impact on skier circulation at Vail. They are so inviting, so big and beautiful, that a lot of "good" skiers now head for the back and simply stay there all day. I sympathize, and have been known to do just that myself, but it's still an under-utilization of Vail's vast resources. Why not set yourself the easy-to-achieve goal of making each Vail day different than the last?

Once you've explored the less demanding lines in *China* and *Siberia Bowls*, and want to venture into Vail's two Classic Bowls, I'd recommend skiing the *Slot* into *Sun Up Bowl* first. Despite their names, *Sun Up Bowl* has no monopoly on early morning light, nor does *Sun Down* get great sunsets. Like the New Bowls, there aren't any traditional cut runs back here at all, only generalized lines that have been given separate names. And although all these lines are all marked black on the Vail trail map, some are much blacker than others. The *Slot* is the only run in the Classic Bowls that's ever machine groomed. Since, both *Sun Down* and *Sun Up* are more suitable for expert and near expert skiers, I'll describe them in more detail in the next section.

Your day will have a very different feel if you start out on the Lionshead side of the mountain. One look at the trail map shows you that the runs on the western end of Vail Mountain are quite long and that there is hardly any black showing over here. The finest runs in Lionshead are are the longest and most continuous ones on the far western edge of the mountain, especially *Simba* with its branches and variants, *Safari* and *Cheetah*. These runs are almost too easy to merit being marked blue for their whole length, but their sweep and width, and the continuous non-stop quality of skiing over here gives them a special feeling that shorter runs of the same difficulty lack. After Vail's first massive infusion of high-speed quad lifts for the 85/86 season, skiers rapidly became spoiled by the no-lift-line conditions on the middle and upper sections of Vail Mountain. Transportation bottlenecks on the Lionshead side seemed so frustrating that knowledgeable skiers just didn't bother to ski over here much. All this has changed with the new Born Free Express quad replacing old lift 8. If you're in reasonably good shape, try to ski these long Lionshead runs non-stop, top to bottom; or at least in longer sections than normal. Pure exhilaration.

Cruising is a sport, or addiction, best practiced on newly groomed runs –"virgin corduroy" as some call it, referring to the patterns made in the snow by the grooming vehicles' big rollers. At Vail you can lift any mountain telephone and dial 4018 to get a prerecorded report telling you which slopes have been groomed the night before.

VAIL FOR EXPERTS

There is still a certain lingering snobbishness in Colorado ski circles which insists that while Vail is a great cruising mountain for average skiers, real experts will sooner or later get bored there. Nonsense! Vail is not one of those mountains whose trail map looks like a forbidding grill of black bars, but with its enormous size, it still has more serious expert runs than most other mountains in Colorado. This expert skiing comes in two flavors: steep, fierce bump skiing and ungroomed, all-terrain, all-snow skiing, mostly on the back side. A day in the Back Bowls in fresh powder is the finest experience Vail has to offer.

Bump skiing isn't everyone's cup of tea, but moguled runs are a daily challenge that few expert skiers can resist. At Vail, you'll encounter the challenge of the steep and lumpy in two main areas: chair 10, and Prima.

Chair 10 is bump city. Its three main runs, *Blue Ox*, *Highline* and *Roger's* deserve their double black diamond designation. *Blue Ox* is the easiest of the lot and so, the first one to try if you're hesitating. *Highline*, right under the lift, is the steepest and most continuous, the best long, pure bump run in Vail. That's where you'll see the hot young bumpers with their 20-year-old knees pounding the fall line. This is straightforward, clean bump skiing on big, well-shaped moguls down an obvious fall line, with plenty of width and options for changing lines. In short it's a beaut, unlike the third run, *Roger's* (pronounced Roh-jhay's after early Vail Ski School director, Roger Staub). *Roger's* leads you leftward to the bottom of lift 11, is very narrow at the start and generally messy. This run could be greatly improved by discreet widening and the elimination of a couple of obnoxious tree islands.

Skiing down from the very top of Vail Mountain along the wide boulevard of *Swingsville Ridge*, one eventually comes to a fork: on the left the friendly steeps of *Riva*, and on the right, *Prima*, Vail's classic bump run. Such a classic, in fact, that the Ski School still awards Prima Pins to students who manage to ski it with a bit of grace and composure. The first major steep on *Prima* is called *Brown's Face*. The left side of *Brown's Face* lays back at a slightly gentler angle attracting the majority of skiers; but I find the skiing much better on the far right where the bumps are bigger, smoother, above all more rounded. Below *Brown's Face* you can take a short cut back to chair 11 by taking the *Pronto* cut off. *(Bump specialists, on their way from the top of Vail mountain over to chair 10 and Highline, ski what they call PPL, a killer combination of Prima, Pronto, and Logchute.)* But I don't recommend *Pronto* for mere mortals. The bumps (or more accurately the troughs and gullies) on this short steep face are gnarly and gouged beyond belief. Although only marked black, not double black, I find Pronto to be the meanest, most technically difficult skiing at Vail. Most skiers, even most experts, would do better to follow *Trans Montane* catwalk back around to lift 11. *Prima Cornice*, an extremely steep exit near the top of *Prima*, is surely the most scary, and "serious"run at Vail; in low snow years it often remains closed because the cliff bands aren't sufficiently covered. Don't even consider it unless a steep pitch like *South Rim Run* seems easy.

But for true experts, much of the magic of Vail mountain is found in the Classic Bowls. Other Colorado areas like Winter Park's Mary Jane, Aspen Mountain and Telluride also have terrific bumps; but there are no other Back Bowls. I've skied the Back Bowls in every condition, every season. If you're good, they're always good. But there is nonetheless a sort of hierarchy of adventures back here, lines to ski first, lines for later. And on stormy whiteout days, forget the Back Bowls, you might as well be elsewhere where you can see.

Sun Down and *Sun Up Bowls* are separated by a massive central ridge. The lines on either side ultimately lead you down to roads that take you back to lift 5. The action is all over when you reach these catwalks, so be sure to look around and enjoy the view. *Sun Up Cat-walk*, in particular, brings you round a corner to a sudden splendid view of the peaks of the Holy Cross Wilderness framed between two snowy ridges: Vail's most dramatic alpine view.

If you enter the Classic Bowls through the first gate east of the chair 5 lift line, you'll find yourself skiing along the flat top of the central ridge, *High Noon Ridge*, for a few hundred yards. *(All of Vail's bowls, by the way, are separately controlled areas that one enters through marked gates in roped-off control fences; generally they close earlier than the front side of the mountain to give skiers a chance to get back up and down to the Village by a reasonable hour.)* The slopes leading down and left from this central ridge are the first ones to hit on a Vail powder morning; they're steep, direct and delicious, easy to get to, and they get tracked up quickly. You arrive first at *Milt's Face* (which pretty much represents the whole side or flank of this ridge) and then at *Cow's Face* (the obvious nose at the end of this ridge). There is no correct, or best, place to drop off this ridge: simply turn and dive off where there are few or no tracks. Skiing here is so wide and free that it's quite vague where one named zone stops and the next starts (trail maps, for example, indicate an area between *Milt's* and *Cow's Faces* called *Campbells*, but most long-time Vail skiers won't recognize the name or the spot). There's room for at least a hundred sets of non-overlapping tracks out here. Make one or two sets and head for less popular areas in the Back.

Next in ease of access, less steep but just as broad and even longer is the left side of *Sun Down Bowl* immediately west of the chair 5 lift line. Close to the central ridge this line is called *Forever*, further right into the bowl you'll be skiing *Wow*. Both are best reached by a gate just west of the lift-5 top station which seems to usher you into a narrow tree slot rather than a proper bowl. Not to worry: the trees quickly thin out into a few hundred yards of beautiful glades before disappearing alto-gether at the top of *Forever*.

Because most skiers in the two Classic Bowls seem to circulate in the central area that can be easily reached from chair 5, the many lovely lines on the extreme sides of *Sun Up* and *Sun Down*, don't get skied as much, don't get tracked out as fast, and often yield great powder late in the day, or even a day or two after a snowstorm.

From the ridge between the *Sun Up* and *Tea Cup Bowls* you'll acess *Yonder Gully*, *Yonder*, and *Over Yonder*, wonderful, obscure skiing on the far west-facing flank of *Sun Up Bowl*. This area has a feeling all its own with patchy, wide spaced trees—after *Shangrila*, my favorite

Back Bowl lines on a stormy day.

All the way around, on the opposite, extreme western side of *Sun Down Bowl*, two other remote zones known as *Seldom* and *Never* provide that same, away-from-it-all feeling. You reach *Seldom* and *Never* by entering *Sun Down Bowl* from the top of lift 7 and then traversing all the way right. Other lines on this side like *Morningside Ridge* and *Ricky's Ridge*, also reached from lift 7, provide pretty good skiing but lack the wild character of the Classic Bowls at their best.

Finally there are some mysterious lines in the two Classic Bowls that few skiers ever seem to find. *Windows* is a non-starter; in the four years I spent at Vail, I skied it only a few times and never managed to have a great run. You have to ski down *Minturn Mile* from the top, turn left at the *Windows* gate, bushwhack through a dense unpleasant forest and when you come out in the open, you wind up with a much abbreviated version of *Wow*. Not worth it.

Quite the opposite are two of the finest lines in the Back: *Apres Vous* and *Chicken Yard*. To find *Apres Vous*, head for *Cow's Face* and hug the right-side control fence which takes you around the corner to a hidden face. This is *Apres Vous*, a triangular face that often has a gentle cornice wave at its crest and typically receives deeper wind-drifted snow than the rest of *Sun Up Bowl*. The beauty of *Apres Vous* is not so much the skiing, which is splendid, but the sensation of being out of sight of everything and everyone else in the Back. Eventually this hidden face narrows into a gully that cuts through sparse aspen forests down to the *Sun Up Catwalk*. Even wilder and more isolated is *Chicken Yard*, a second hidden slope that you reach by once again hugging the right side of the *Apres-Vous* control fence and ducking through a marked gate in the ropes. This gate existed for many years before Vail finally put *Chicken Yard* on its trail maps. At the top of this run one has the peculiar sensation of being suspended high above the valley floor that only convex, fall-away terrain conveys ("Like the belly of a pregnant woman," a French roommate of mine used to say). Despite this suspended-in-the-sky feeling, *Chicken Yard* isn't really too steep; the hardest moment comes in the exit gully which is barred by small cliffs. When there isn't enough snow to negotiate the cliffs, the patrol simply closes the *Chicken Yard* gate.

Another great bit of expert-only terrain that many skiers never find is the *Ouzo Glade* (or the *Ouzo Trees*), located not in the Back but in Game Creek Bowl. Use the *Eagle's Nest Ridge* entrance to *Ouzo* and then traverse right for a hundred yards or so on a grooming road before peeling down into the forest. There are many lines here, with continual surprise openings in the trees. In winter the snow is fantastic in these trees, but on spring afternoons it turns heavy because of its direct western exposure.

Vail Mountain is a more intriguing playground for expert skiers than many believe. Not only because of its hard runs. Not only for the Back Bowls. But above all because of the sheer amount of non-stop skiing available. There is enough terrain here, both obvious and hidden, to keep your sense of discovery and surprise alive for seasons. The only reason for one Vail ski day to resemble another is lack of imagination.

VAIL FOR LESS EXPERIENCED SKIERS

Inexperienced skiers, emerging novices, sub-intermediates — skiers who lack either mileage or confidence or both can still have a great time on this mountain. But in all honesty, Vail's choices for this level of skier are somewhat limited. You can wind up spending a lot of time on fairly boring catwalks. Novices and "emerging intermediates" will probably enjoy themselves more, and certainly make more progress if they spend a few days skiing at Vail's sister area, Beaver Creek where they'll find more ideal terrain.

If you're a somewhat better than an emerging novice but still not a very experienced skier, cheer up, you won't feel out of it for long. While you're working on new skills, remember the following lifts and runs: The very best gentle skiing at Vail is served by lifts 3, 7 and 14; although you'll have to take some other lifts (and ski down some other runs) to take full advantage of these hyper-friendly zones.

In my opinion, the finest run for inexperienced skiers on Vail mountain is *Lost Boy*, the left-hand ridge run of *Game Creek Bowl*. It's long and flatish, but still feels like a big mountain experience. Cruise *Lost Boy* to your heart's content, it's the only good run in *Game Creek* for inexperienced skiers, but when you leave chair 7 be sure to turn left down *Eagles' Nest Ridge*. Then you can either return to Mid-Vail via *The Meadows, Jake's Jaunt* or *Over Easy*; or continue on down *Eagle's Nest Ridge* to the LionsHead side of the mountain. From Mid-Vail, less experienced skiers should start down the mountain on *Lion's Way*, a gentle packed road. When this road ends, a series of broad open slopes (where runs like *Pickeroon* and *Berries* dead-end in flats) will steer you down toward the top of chair 1 and the loading maze of the Avanti Express quad. From here, follow *Gitalong Road* back to Vail Village (skiing sections of *Bear Tree* when you cross them – if they look groomed and inviting). Or, if you're heading home to Lionshead, continue traversing across the mountain when you pass *Bear Tree* and you will wind up on *Born Free*, the main drag down into Lionshead. Hesitant skiers should avoid the one steep spot here by following a trail marked *Village Catwalk* into the forest and back in a long zigzag which takes one around the last steep pitch on lower *Born Free*.

I've already said that *The Far East* is also a real novice skier's paradise. All runs on chair 14 are optimal for inexperienced, learning skiers. The only flaw here is the trip home, which necessitates taking *Flapjack* all the way to the bottom of lift 11 (*Flapjack* is easy if it's been recently groomed, daunting if not – so ask an instructor). From the bottom of lift 11, you'll slide down *Skid Road* to the backside loading station of lift 6, and from the top of 6, ski an easy blue, *Ruder's Run* back to the Village. If there's a line on the backside of lift 6, you can escape via the aptly named *South 6 Escape* (but otherwise this run is too boring).

Already, you may have spotted Vail Mountain's only real weakness. Extremely inexperienced skiers tend to spend a lot of time on roads and catwalks. The reverse side of the coin is that you won't stay inexperienced for long on such a friendly mountain.

Supposing, however, that without being a very strong skier, you are pretty good at coping with average blue runs – even though you don't "bomb" them the way I assumed that "good skiers" did. In that case, you have a lot more choices. Around Mid-Vail start with *Swingsville*, it's neighbor *Christmas*, and *Ramshorn* (all marked green but actually easy blue in difficulty). I'd also recommend several beautiful cruising runs on the Middle Mountain: *Avanti* and *Pickeroon*. Each has one steep black face, but you can go around these steep pitches on conveniently provided escape paths. Farther west, you should try *Columbine* and *Ledges*. Finally, the westernmost run on the whole mountain, *Simba*, is easy, wide and inviting for most of the way down (until you reach *Post Road*). It's marked blue, but no one would argue if it were green. When you hit Post Road, follow it right to *Born Free* and you'll be home free.

VAIL FOR BEGINNERS

Vail has two separate beginner areas on different sides of the mountain. There is a difference between them, and you should take this into account when deciding where you or your friends will start learning how to ski on Vail mountain.

On the Village side, first-time and beginner classes meet at Golden Peak, and will soon be riding chair 12. This chair serves an area that's nicely roped off from traffic but is still, for a rank beginner, a bit steep. Yet as a result of this robust practice environment, beginners who learn at Golden Peak are better prepared for what in Vail is called the "first-day mountain" experience – skiing the whole mountain, top to bottom.

Lionshead beginners, by contrast, are taken right to the top on the gondola, and make their first moves on the wonderful, gentle slopes of chair 15. A nearly effortless experience. The rub is that chair 15 is too easy; so beginners who learn up there are often not well prepared for their first full-mountain experience. Lionshead instructors therefore have cunningly put together the absolutely easiest way down their side of the mountain, combining bits and pieces of various runs into what they call "the teaching trail." If you're looking for an extremely gentle way down the mountain from Eagle's Nest, here it is: At the bottom of chair 15, turn right onto *Owl's Roost*. Follow this catwalk straight across several steeper bluish runs like upper *Ledges* and *Lodgepole*, till it turns a sharp corner and zigs back across the same runs, leading you into the middle or green section of *Ledges*. This series of gentle pitches around small tree islands leads you to another road, *Cub's Way*, which you'll follow rightwards to the top of chair 1. From there, *Gitalong Road* takes you home to the bottom of the mountain. It's a mighty roundabout journey, but it works, even for those who can barely stand up on skis.

SPECIAL PROGRAMS, SPECIAL TIPS

Vail boasts the largest ski school in the country, and certainly one of the best. I was quite proud to instruct there for a number of years, in the blue uniform with the black and white diagonal stripes that Roger Staub made famous. But all ski school programs are not created equal, even at Vail. A few recommendations:

Vail's children's ski school is incredible, the best I've seen, any-where. In fact, there are actually a number of kids'ski schools and special programs. Starting with *Small World*, a nursery for youngsters from 2 months to two and a half years, kids graduate into Mogul Mice and then Super Stars. There are splendid child-care facilities at both Golden Peak and Lionshead, from which the littlest ones can forge out for short introductions to skiing, or leave in more experienced groups for longer runs when they're ready. The recently constructed Children's Ski Center at Golden Peak is is a modern two-story kids' palace. The "regular" kids' ski school teaches children from 6 up; and finally, teen-agers are grouped in their own classes. In recent years the children's ski school has been the most creative branch of this giant school, and has developed an amazing Children's Adventure program on Vail mountain. A unique kids' trail map (see page 32) outlines a multitude of special

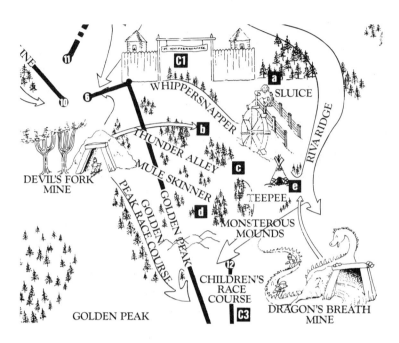

This small excerpt from the 1988 Vail/Beaver Creek children's trail map shows some of the activities and discoveries awaiting small skiers in the Golden Peak area of Vail mountain. (Reproduced courtesy of Vail Associates.)

children's activities and kids' ski school programs, and points the way to mysterious mine shafts designed for young skiers to explore, Indian villages and burial grounds, a mountain lion's den, and more. The children' program on this mountain is as much a contribution to tomorrow's skiing as all Vail's quad chairs.

How about adults? I'm less sanguine about the quality of grownup instruction here for a curious reason. Vail has the largest and most affluent private lesson clientele of any North American ski mountain. (Of three ski school base locations, one, in the heart of Vail Village, specializes in private lessons exclusively.) Since instructors make a far better living teaching privates than group lessons, all the hot instructor talent at Vail winds up booked for the season with private lessons. Well and good, if you can afford the tab (upwards from $60 per hour, or upwards from $300 for an all-day private). But an unfortunate side-effect is that instructors teaching group lessons on Vail mountain are apt to be less experienced, less motivated and less skilled. The chances of getting a great group lesson here are correspondingly low.

Another ski school program, however merits a special word. Super Class, out of Vail Village, is a day-long, non-stop, guided-tour of hard skiing for very strong skiers. If you find the sheer size and multiple possibilities of Vail mountain confusing, then Super Class may be for you. No instruction, but loads of skiing behind someone who knows the mountain inside and out, and whose job is to share the best it has to offer.

While bottlenecks and crowding are no longer a problem during a day's skiing on Vail Mountain, the same can't be said of the classical crunch as skiers return to the valley in the evening. Mountain Hostesses and Hosts are pressed into service to direct homeward traffic and help keep speed down. And you'll wish there was another way to get down in the evening. There is. In fact there are several. In Lionshead, most skiers ski home via *Born Free*, but instead I'd recommend *The Glade*, one of the most delightful, semi-hidden spots on Vail mountain. *The Glade* is a series of openings in a beautiful aspen forest that's usually half-deserted when *Born Free* is choked with bodies. If you're a strong skier, there are short black pitches into Lionshead that avoid the evening congestion; it's also more pleasant to ski home on the western side of the gondola line, following lower *Simba*, than on *Born Free*.

To return to Vail Village in the evening, sans crowds, I recommend the same route. Head for for the Lionshead side, ski *The Glade*, and when you emerge on the last shoulder of *Born Free*, take *Village Cat-walk* all the way back across to the Village.

In stormy weather forget most of the Back Bowls. Visibility is so marginal without trees, that it isn't worth it. But the *Shangrila* trees in China Bowl are a delightful exception. In fact, the lower mountain is better than the upper ridges. The lower, Lionshead side of the mountain really comes into its own in storms. For one thing, you can ride the gondola and really stay warm and dry; for another, the timber on this side of the mountain is denser and so the runs not only feel more sheltered, but your visibility will be at a maximum. The basic strategy for a stormy day, anywhere, is to ski *right next* to the trees and avoid the featureless center sections of wider slopes.

LUNCH TIME

I've already given Vail Mountain enough sincere, well deserved praise that I don't feel the least bit negative when I tell you the best lunches on Vail mountain are actually in the Village, or in Lionshead, below.

Food service on the mountain is certainly adequate. But the food is resolutely institutional, that is to say, mediocre. And Vail's mountain restaurants, whether cafeteria style or sit-down, simply lack charm. When a ski resort is as hot as Vail, you have to compare it with the best around, and for my money, that means European mountain food service, which is in a whole different league.

However, there's an easy alternative to mass-produced mountain grub. Ski down and eat lunch in any number of fine eateries off the mountain. This never used to be an option for serious skiers, because getting back up the mountain after lunch wasted too much time. The age of high-speed quads has changed that. Long Middle Mountain runs like *Avanti* or *Lodgepole* are totally empty around noon, as are lower *Prima* and *Riva*. You'll be down in a flash. You can enjoy a far better lunch at better prices downtown, and be back up on top of the mountain in plenty of time to wear your legs to a frazzle long before the lifts close.

If you're in the mood for a really romantic lunch up on the mountain, and the weather looks good, I'd recommend picking up a classic French *pique-nique* (in a small backpack) from *Les Delices de France* in Lionshead, and enjoying it, with a bottle of Beaujolais, on one of the many mountain picnic decks that are marked on the trail map. My favorite deck is at Wildwood, overlooking Sun Down Bowl.

The lunchtime "scene" on the mountain, however, is the Cook Shack, a sit-down restaurant under the Mid-Vail building. My earlier comments about food and atmosphere apply to the Cook Shack too, but this little enclave of Vail society is still worth checking out, if only for their Mortal Sin dessert, and for the sight of so many stockbrokers and bankers eating lunch with so many private instructors. The number of instructors per table is one of Vail's key tokens of conspicuous consumption. In certain circles the Cook Shack is such an important place to be seen that reservations for the Christmas holiday period are sometimes made a year in advance – Vail's version of the "power lunch."

AROUND TOWN, VAIL AMBIANCE

The town of Vail has grown up in 25 years from less than modest beginnings (a single homestead in a green and grassy valley) to an alpine urban center with three (count them!) exits from the freeway (I-70) that runs through the valley, linking Denver with Grand Junction and points west. It's really a small mountain city more than a town or a village, but despite its size and bustle it's still a remarkable place to spend a ski vacation.

For one thing, unlike many ski resorts (to which Gertrude Stein's classic comment about Oakland, "There's no there, there." applies all too well) Vail has a real center, two centers actually, which give a human and commercial hub to town life. Vail bashing is a popular activity at other Colorado ski towns, where folks complain about Vail's ticky-tacky instant atmosphere and its imitation Tyrolean architecture. I'd say they're all wet. Such comments come more from jealousy than judgment. The architecture does have alpine overtones, ranging from subtle woodwork and rounded chimney-cap details to cartoon-like pastiche. But in fact, it's a good deal more tasteful, and authentic in the sense of being true to itself than a lot of recently built ski villages I've visited in the Alps. I like it.

Vail Village is more intriguing than Lionshead, which is understand-able, since it's some ten years older. Both town centers are true pedes-trian zones, where life and living people, not cars and exhaust fill the streets. I've already said that Vail is the *only* true pedestrian ski village in North America, and this is a major part of its success. Vail has banished America's worst urban plague, the automobile, to the outskirts of town, and to the outer reaches of vacationing visitors' consciousness. If you bring your car to Vail (which certainly isn't necessary), you're going to park it and forget it for the rest of the week. And love living without it.

Both Vail Village and Lionshead are so crammed full of shops, boutiques, galleries, eateries and lodges, you'll need a week to explore the place – and you'll need a lot of money to take advantage of it all too. The price of success, this much success, is price. And Vail is as pricey as they come with *nouveau riche* overtones that are so up-front they don't really offend. The flow of people and commerce in Vail Village sweeps you along Bridge Street (which runs from the landmark Covered Bridge, beneath a totally hidden, three-story, underground parking structure, uphill to the Vista Bahn). Bridge Street is the axis of social life in the Vail Village. Within half a block you'll find the two most chic sport/fashion stores, Gorsuch and Pepi's, too many designer fur shops, and all the ritz and glitz of a big time resort. But Vail Village isn't a one-block shopping stop either. There are back streets, arcades, tucked-away courtyards, shops that will take you more than one or two evenings to find.

The apres-ski scene on this side of town is a little more intense than it is in LionsHead. And you'll soon discover the basic Vail Village pub crawl, known around town as the "Bridge Street Shuffle." Los Amigos is the slopeside center of the nachos and Margarita set, and its deck is wall-to-wall bodies on spring afternoons. In fact, the finest apres-ski show in town is the view of the Gore Range turning rose and purple in late evening Alpenglow, high over town.

To get from Vail Village to Lionshead, or vice versa, indeed to get around period, you'll want to use Vail's free town shuttle bus system. It'll take you only one ride to get oriented. The town loop is continuous and obvious, and even very young kids use these buses to navigate Vail on their own. Between the Village and Lionshead, there is a key bus stop for the Dobson Ice Arena (public skating at various hours as well as fierce local hockey action). The trip from one side of Vail to the other is only about five minutes.

Lionshead is a more free-form resort center, with open plazas and stairways rather than an actual grid of streets defining its spaces and circulation. There is more lodging, more condos and condotels, on the Lionshead side than over in Vail Village, so it's never empty even though, as I mentioned, the Village side seems to offer more in the way of shopping and apres ski.

DINING AND LODGING IN VAIL

In a few of the Colorado ski resorts covered in this guide one really has to search to get a fine meal. This is not exactly the problem in either of our first two resorts, Vail and Aspen. Here the problem is one of an embarrassment of riches. So instead of listing all the good restaurants in town, I'm going to do something quite rash, talk only about my personal favorites.

My absolute number one choice for dinner in Vail is Sweet Basil: a tastefully decorated, low-key sort of "California nouveau" restaurant that is definitely neither the most expensive nor the most elegant place to eat. Sweet Basil simply serves the most consistently interesting cooking in town. Which is a hell of a compliment considering the competition!

Two consistent locals's favorites are Blu's – best described as an eclectic American bistro – and Ludwig's an Austro-Germanic style res- taurant in the Sonnenalp Hotel (of which more anon) which serves an extravagent breakfast buffet every day.

There are a number of fairly classic French and Frenchified restau- rants at Vail, of which the Left Bank is the best known. But I find these restaurants too predictable – slightly too elegant service, slightly too expensive prices, slightly too familiar menus – rather than wonderful culinary surprises.

Dinning out in Minturn, on the contrary, is something you'll remem- ber for a while. Minturn is a scruffy, true-grit sort of town, ten minutes from Vail, tucked away in a side canyon under the rocky crag that gave

Lionshead its name. A town which owes its existence and half its
redneck and Latino population to its railroad yards. Here you'll want to
check out The Minturn Country Club, a funky, cook-your-own-steak
emporium, and the Saloon, a giant, barn-like Mexican restaurant. Both
are long-time local favorites, both provide an entertaining counterpart to
more formal Vail dining.

I hope you'll forgive me for being even less exhaustive about Vail
accommodations than about its restaurants. Your choice of good lodging is, if anything, greater and broader than that of good food. Naturally
Vail has a "system" to lodge its guests (see the Vail Data section.) in
anything from very posh full-service hotels, through luxury apartments
to quite basic ski-resort condos.

But I have two personal favorites to pass along, chosen for atmosphere, architecture and charm: the Sonnenalp Hotel and the Christiania
Lodge. The Christiania is definitely "old Vail;" it stands at the foot of
the slopes in Vail Village and its old-fashioned bar/lounge is surely the
least trendy apres-ski rendezvous in Vail. The Sonnenalp, next to the
Covered Bridge, feels like "old Vail" but actually the building was a
dismal motel-like structure in the early days which has been miracu-
lously remodeled into a masterpiece of authentic Austro-alpine wooden
carpentry.

Lodging a bit out of town (say on the other side of the I-70 freeway
which bisects the valley, or slightly west in the direction of the bedroom
community of Eagle-Vail) costs somewhat less than staying right in
Lionshead or Vail Village. But I must say, despite its outrageously
deluxe reputation (and its outrageously deluxe reality), most Vail
lodging is comparably priced with similar lodging in other Colorado ski
areas. Many of the outlying lodging complexes offer their own shuttle-
van transport to and from the center, so you can still enjoy the pedestrian
quality of a Vail vacation. Skiers staying at, or near, the Westin Hotel
way out in West Vail, even get to use a special lift, chair 20, The Cascade Village Lift, which was built exclusively to connect this outlying
district with *Simba* and the LionsHead trail system. A comeback
catwalk, *Westin Ho!*, brings you home when the lifts have closed.

VAIL DATA

Snow Conditions		(303) 476-48
	also:	(303) 476-4889
Ski Area Information		1-800-525-22
	also:	(303) 476-5601
Central Reservations		1-800-525-225
	also:	1-800-525-3875

TRANSPORTATION

By car, 2 hour drive (in good road and weather conditions) from Denver on I-70. There are 3 Vail exits.

By bus or limo, from Denver's Stapleton Airport.

By plane, via Continental Express to the STOL-port at Avon; private planes must land at the Eagle County Airport, approximately 30 miles from Vail.

MOUNTAIN STATISTICS

Vertical Drop	3,250 feet
Summit Elev.	11,450 feet
Base Elevation	8,200 feet
Skiing Terrain	3,787 acres
Number of Lifts	20 including, 7 high-speed detachable quad chairs, one gondola and 2 surface lifts
Uphill Capacity	35,820 skiers per hour
Longest Run	4 miles
Snowboarding	yes (and monoskiing too!)

Vail lift tickets are good at Beaver Creek

SKI TECH: A POWDER PRIMER

Powder skiing is a great liberation – from gravity, from effort, from worldly cares. But you have to defeat the powder paradox first. The paradox is this: once you know how to ski in deep snow, it seems much easier than skiing on the pack; but learning to ski powder is always harder than learning to turn on packed slopes. Here's a simplified method to get you past the frustrations of learning to ski powder as quickly as possible.

Balance first. *Or as I used to tell my students: "stability before mobility." You'll need a new sort of balance in deep snow – standing two-footed, weight roughly equal on both skis. If you stand on one ski, which is the normal mode for hardpack, that weighted ski will dive while the other one floats up, and woops!... To develop two-footed powder balance, be sure you do a bit of straight running and traversing before you start turning downhill in deep snow. Bounce and flex up and down on both skis as you descend in a straight line; and adapt your stance for better balance by spreading your arms wider than normal.*

The powder stance: arms wide, weight equal on both skis.

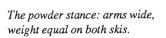

Slow-motion speed control. *Everything takes longer to accomplish in deep snow: skis don't just whip around, they come about slowly, gently. You'll feel as if you are skiing in slow motion. This is normal and is due to the extra resistance from your skis being buried inside the snow, rather than just sliding over the top of it. Get used to finishing turns gently — pulling smoothly out of the fall line much slower than normal. A jerky attempt to pivot your skis sideways in powder will inevitably produce a fall. From a steep traverse sink down, then slowly, smoothly twist your skis uphill while extending your legs and pushing/ grinding your heels sideways. Twisting extension is the key to a strong finish for a powder turn.*

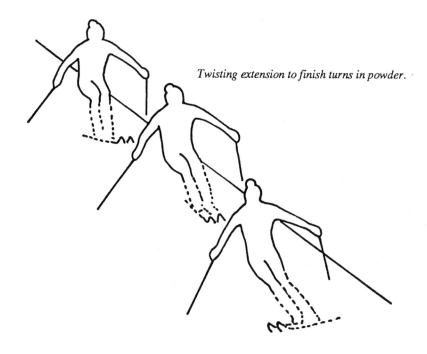

Twisting extension to finish turns in powder.

Launching your turns down the hill. *Here we have another powder paradox: for experienced powder skiers, short linked turns are easiest, but newcomers will find that individual medium to long-radius turns give more success. Launch these turns by using a couple of "powder tricks," either separately or together. The first trick is to vigorously lift your outside hand as you start your turn . This will help to unweight the fronts of your skis and banks you neatly in the diection of the turn – a real secret weapon in extremely deep snow. And a big help*

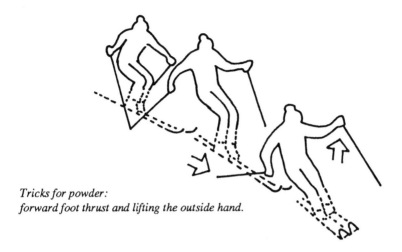

Tricks for powder:
forward foot thrust and lifting the outside hand.

when you're learning. The other trick is more subtle. If it works for you, great! If not, don't give it a second thought. I'm talking about pushing both feet forward as you start your turn. This is a hard-to-observe move, but believe me, good powder skiers do it a lot, often subconsciously. By thrusting both feet forward in the direction of the new turn down the hill, you will be guaranteeing equal weight on both skis...and once again, helping to lighten the fronts of the skis.

And please, don't be too demanding, too judgmental about your own performance on your first few excursions into powder snow. Falling is inevitable and, with the right attitude, almost fun. At first, surviving turns in the deep – just staying on your feet – is more important than doing them right. After you've proved to yourself that you can make it down a slope covered with a foot and a half of fluff, it's easier to find the confidence to work out the details, to ski the same slope, better, smoother, more gracefully. Like everything else on skis, powder skiing is a progression. Remember the sequence: first develop a new type of balance on two feet, two skis; then a slow-motion finish to your turns; finally a powerful "lifting" start to launch them.

Soon you'll be connecting medium-radius turns through knee-deep powder that used to psych you out. At first you shouldn't try to link turns too closely – that will be the final step. You'll want to use the space between turns to catch your breath, smile in amazement that you made it, and get yourself together for that next turn. Already, after your first few successes, you'll know why skiers rave about powder. It really is the ultimate. It is very close to flying!

CHAPTER 2   BEAVER CREEK

Vail's little sister, Beaver Creek – just a short drive down the Eagle river valley – is finally growing up into an attractive teenager, but it's not yet a mature beauty one can fall in love with. After a slow start, Beaver Creek now turns in some pretty impressive statistics. In terms of skier visits, uphill capacity, mountain facilities, vertical drop, and a number of other yardsticks by which such things are measured, it is now a major ski resort. Last year the Vail Valley (which means Vail and Beaver Creek) successfully hosted the FIS world championships; and Beaver Creek was the site of the most prestigious event, the men's' downhill. It was in the spotlight of world TV coverage, groomed and buffed to a high luster for its international debut. The message was clear Beaver Creek is coming on strong.

But honestly, in my opinion, it's not yet there. In many ways, this ski resort today has the same polish, the same level of service and expertise as Vail, but the experience just isn't comparable. Most skiers won't find the slopes as satisfying. Beaver Creek is not merely smaller than Vail, its skiing is one-dimensional and overly predictable when compared to Vail's stunning diversity. Although, as we'll see in this chapter, there are a couple of skiing dimensions in which Beaver Creek not only rivals but surpasses its older sister. And the village – well, in a word the village lacks soul. It is simply too artificial, too exclusively oriented toward the super rich to seem genuine. (A forbidding entrance gate to the valley where all but property owners are turned back to take a shuttle bus is not *my* idea of a warm welcome.)

Actually I'm an optimist. I'm fairly certain that enough time and enough work will turn Beaver Creek into a masterpiece of a ski resort, even though nature hasn't blessed it with anything resembling the Back Bowls. It can still grow up into a raving beauty. For now I recommend that you profit from one or two days at Beaver Creek to vary your Vail ski vacation. Your Vail lift ticket will work here, and transportation between the two mountains is easy. But better wait a few more years before taking Beaver Creek seriously.

THE LAY OF THE LAND, VALLEY AND MOUNTAIN

You don't just drive up to Beaver Creek and go skiing. The area is located at the upper end of a steep side valley, that enters the larger Eagle River valley by the new town of Avon, a few miles west of Vail on I-70. Avon is part of my frustration and disappointment with Beaver Creek. It was built at the same time as the ski area, built but seemingly neither planned nor designed, and today is a hodgepodge bedroom community, full of parking lots and cars. A place where a pedestrian would be risking his or her life to go for a walk, if there was anything worth walking to. Like Dillon and Silverthorne over in Summit County, Avon is lowest-common-denominator, shopping-center development imported into the mountains. Pity. Up at the head of the canyon, Beaver Creek's mini village is a hundred times nicer; but it's too small, too pricey, and in the last analysis, too uniformly tasteful (as if everything were cast from the same mold) to rival Vail's diverse almost-urban mosaic. Both Avon and Beaver Creek "work" in different ways. Avon provides lots of affordable even low-budget housing near two super ski areas, especially for Vail Valley locals; while Beaver Creek's base provides the spiffy luxury accommodations – but the whole picture doesn't add up to a harmonious whole, a memorable ski town that's greater than the sum of its amenities. Never mind, we're going skiing.

Unless you're staying at Beaver Creek, or riding the bus from Vail, you have to park in a large lot at the mouth of the canyon and take a shuttle bus up to the area. The shuttles leave every few minutes and the ride is a fairly short one. Up at the base you'll be looking in two directions. There's the main mountain straight ahead of you. A spacious beginner pasture at the bottom and a quad chair charging right up the center of a massive rounded peak where ribbon runs alternate with dark evergreen forests. On your right, another chair rises through open aspens up what looks like a different mountain.

And that's Beaver Creek in a nutshell: a massive central ridge, essentially "two lifts high." The Centennial Express quad carries you most of the way up, to the large mid-mountain restaurant at Spruce Saddle, and from there a triple takes you on to the top. The top of the mountain is as gentle as can be, and another chair slanting up from the east serves a fantastic network of easy forgiving novice trails. Further down the east side of this big ridge, a recent lift, chair 4 serves a slanting

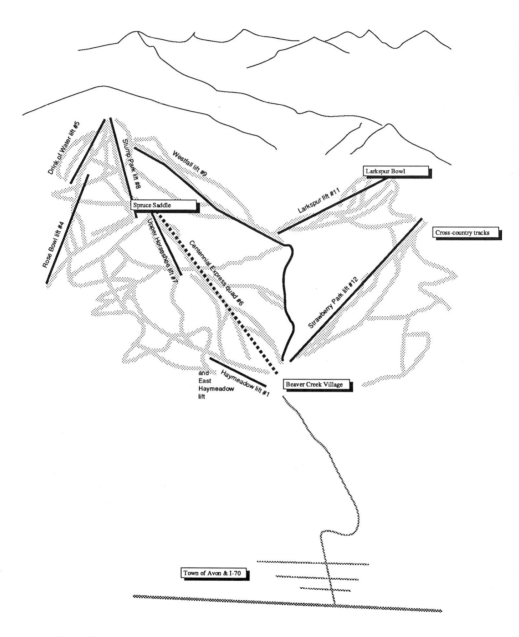

*Beaver Creek—
a sketch map showing
lifts and main runs. For
details, consult the current area trail map
which indicates the names and difficulty of all runs.*

side-drainage called *Rose Bowl*. While on the opposite, western side of
the ridge, chair 9 serves Beaver Creek's most serious terrain, the three
Birds of Prey runs, *Golden Eagle, Peregrine* and *Goshawk*.

Then to the west of all this, across a creek-bed drainage, there's a
second smaller mountain, that for the moment is served by only two
chairs, one from the base, and one higher up the valley connecting with
the bottom of lift 9 and the Birds of Prey. Its slopes are bathed in early
morning light and have a very different feel from those on the main side
of the mountain: light and airy like the pale aspen forests around them.
On top of this "side mountain" is another surprise: Colorado's most
unusual cross-country ski area, about which I'll tell you more soon.
Let's look closer.

BEAVER CREEK FOR BEGINNERS
& LESS EXPERIENCED SKIERS

This is the class of skiers that will absolutely go crazy over this area.
There's much more suitable and intriguing skiing terrain for novices
here than at Vail itself. That famous "first-day mountain" experience,
where skiers leave the cradle, forgo the comfort of the beginner slope
and go on up the mountain like everyone else, that first big step is a snap
at Beaver Creek. Novices here get to go to the very top. Ski on runs
like *Red Buffalo, Booth Gardens* and *Powell*, all morning long, gentle
barely inclined rivers of snow. And then take *Cinch* or *Dally* back to the
bottom. Without a traumatic moment.

It's not that the whole mountain is flat, quite the contrary. Simply
that there is so much gentle skiing at the very top, and that the easy
descent roads are so well designed and groomed. *Cinch* is just that, a
big road, but it doesn't have a cramped, narrow "catwalk" feel. Beaver
Creek is a novice skiers dream. Also, I'd guess that you can get a better
group lesson here than you can at Vail. This is because the Beaver
Creek ski school (which like the rest of the mountain staff here is really
an extension of the Vail original) hasn't yet developed the amazing
private lesson clientele that Vail has, so you are more likely to find top
instructors teaching group lessons.

I should add that while it's the easy upper-mountain terrain that
makes Beaver Creek such a standout for novice and learning skiers,
first-timers here are well served too. The Haymeadow beginner area at
the base village has recently been expanded with the addition of a new
double chair, the East Haymeadow lift.

BEAVER CREEK FOR GOOD SKIERS

What does Beaver Creek offer good skiers? A very straightforward gradation of terrain, steady pitches and excellent grooming (dial 4602 on any mountain phone for a grooming report), no nasty surprises, no blue runs suddenly turning black and ugly and, for the most part, uncrowded and reasonably wide slopes. I'm hesitating on this last point because not all the slopes at Beaver Creek are as wide as I'd like to see them, nor as wide as most slopes at Vail. Particularly the runs underneath *Cinch* on the lower mountain like *Assay*, *Fool's Gold* and *Latigo*, which are all a little harder than the slope would lead you to think, simply because they're narrow. Others like *Centennial* (Beaver Creek's longest run from top to bottom) and especially *Red Tail* (a *Bird of Prey* for the average skier) are absolutely perfect, wide-open sheets of snow where intermediate skiers can stretch their wings and fly. *Red Tail* takes you down to the base of lift 11. This chair climbs the opposite slope, that "second mountain" I talked about earlier, and deposits you at the top of *Larkspur Bowl*. Along with *Red Tail* and *Centennial*, this is the other "perfect" upper-intermediate run on the mountain, very wide, very free, the sort of run on which everyone skis just a little bit better.

The same is not quite true of the "opposite side" runs on lift 12, lower down the mountain. Here the combination of lower altitude and direct eastern sun exposure works against the snow conditions, and runs like *Pitchfork* and *Stacker* often turn icy late in the season.

By the way, if you think you've missed a few lifts in my thumbnail descriptions of how the mountain works, don't worry. The numbering system is based on some eventually to be completed master plan, and although there's even a lift 14 now, there are not yet 14 lifts in total. Patience.

BEAVER CREEK FOR EXPERTS

There are a several steep black pitches on the right bank of *LarkSpur Bowl*, some short steep slots dropping into *Rose Bowl*, and a couple of short black stretches on the lower main mountain. But really, for experts Beaver Creek is synonymous with the *Birds of Prey* and the *Birds of Prey* are synonymous with steep moguls.

A lot of skiers find these runs daunting, harder or at least more awkward than Vail's classic chair-10 bump runs like Highline and Blue Ox. They're not; but they are much narrower, a factor which inhibits even experts. They also tend to get a bit wind-scoured, which can can create some sudden rocky surprises early in the season. *Goshawk* is the shortest of the three and a good run to test yourself on first if you have any doubts. I think Golden Eagle is the most enjoyable. And I have to tell you that these bumps are really good. They don't get skied as hard or as often as similar bump runs at Vail, the gullies don't get pounded into narrow grooves, so you can almost always find good rounded exit lines from every bump. What Beaver Creek seems to lack is a zone of easy consistent practice bumps where skiers can build the skills to negotiate the big bad ones. But this is a problem everywhere. The easy bumps that would be ideal for practicing are also easy to groom away, and have an uncanny habit of disappearing overnight just when they get good. Ah well....

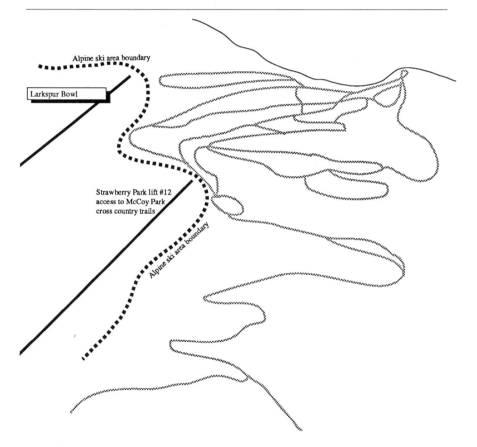

APRES-SKI AND EXTRA SKI IN BEAVER CREEK

The "extra" I want to tell you about is the Nordic trail park on top of lift 12. I realize that not many downhill skiers share my passion for cross-country skiing; and that in the minds of most downhillers, Nordic or cross-country skiing is equated with jogging; or worse with the shuffling timid strides of people who have a pathological fear of sliding and hide in the valley bottoms, while their spouses and friends fly off the summits. It's not necessarily true. For starters at Beaver Creek, they've put the Nordic area on top, where the great views live. It's a real delight just to be there, more so to ski there. And second, cross-country skiing is a new ballgame: something called skating, something that Alpine skiers are generally very good at, has changed the complexion of cross-country forever. It's become a high-speed, gliding, flowing sport. It's a ball. And there's no better, more beautiful place to see what modern cross-country skiing is all about than high above Beaver Creek. Take a "skating" lesson up there and you'll be blown away.

For apres, Beaver style, let me suggest a whole evening. A trip to Beano's Cabin. This is a hideaway up on the ski mountain where the very extravagant dinner begins with a sleigh ride to the cabin. If you can combine dinner at Beano's, good weather and a moonlit night, you've really got something. In the same vein – but even more so – would be an overnight stay at Trapper's Cabin. This very exclusive lodge, also hidden in the forest above Beaver Creek, is designed (and priced) to make you feel like a featured guest on "Lifestyles of the Rich and Famous." If you happen to be rich or famous, or want to splurge for a taste of the experience, this is the place.

BEAVER CREEK DATA

KEY PHONE NUMBERS

Snow Conditions   1-800-525-2257
                  also: (303) 476-4888
                  also: (303) 476-4889

Ski Area Information   1-800-525-2257
                  also: (303) 949-5750

Central Reservations   800-525-2257

TRANSPORTATION

By car, 2 1/2 hour drive (in good road and weather conditions) from Denver on I-70 to the Avon exit, then south 1 mile. Located 1 mile from Avon STOL-port, Beaver Creek is 10 miles west of Vail.

By bus or limo, from Denver's Stapleton Airport, and from the Avon Stolport.

By plane, via Continental Express to the STOL-port at Avon; private planes must land at the Eagle County Airport, approximately 30 miles from Vail.

MOUNTAIN STATISTICS

Vertical Drop	3,340 feet
Summit Elev.	11,440 feet
Base Elevation	8,100 feet
Skiing Terrain	800 acres
Number of Lifts	10 including 1 high-speed detachable quad
Uphill capacity	16,459 skiers/hour
Longest Run	2 3/4 miles
Snowboarding	yes (and monoskiing too!)

This is the age of "parallel" skiing, but it might be more accurate to call it the age of "sloppy parallel" skiing. Nowadays it's easy, easier than ever, to make turns with your skis parallel. In fact, two out of three skiers on the slopes don't do anything special to turn their skis, they just twist 'em around in the direction they want to go. And by twisting both skis more or less together, they pull off more or less parallel turns.

Most intermediate skiers know what I'm talking about. They turn their skis together, but the result is a kind of sloppy, ill-defined, wide-track skid, rather than a graceful carving arc where the two skis slice around in a narrow, elegant track. Parallel turns but not the sort that instructors and experts make. Let's do something about it. The secrets of a polished parallel turn are fewer than you think, and relatively easy to master. The first, critical step is learning to ride the arc of the turn.

This one is easy, if I can convince you to stand exclusively, 100%, on your outside ski. That's right. Average skiers who make rough-and-ready, hit-or-miss parallel skids, skis wide apart, always stand almost equally on both skis. What's the difference? Modern skis are softer in flex than earlier skis; this allows them to bend under the skier's weight (so-called "reverse camber"); and this bent ski is what "carves" a pure round arc in the snow. But in order to make your skis bend, you really have to load them up with maximum weight. Suppose you weigh 150 pounds and stand equally on both skis, then each ski only supports 75 pounds. But if you stand completely over one foot, it's like dropping an additional 75 pound sandbag onto that ski. You've doubled the weight on that ski, and it will bend and carve for you. It's that simple. Modern skis are designed to turn best with the full weight of your body pressing down on only one ski, the outside ski of the turn. (By the way, the reverse bend, or reverse camber, in the ski is hard to observe – you can see it best in still photos – but it's always there in a good turn.)

Skiing with all your weight on the outside ski.

So your first step in mastering modern parallel is to develop the balance needed to put all your weight on one foot. Practice one-footed skiing on gentle flats and catwalks. Lift the light foot up off the snow just to check whether or not you're cheating. Play with the idea, make it a habit. Your turns will improve immediately. And believe it or not, your legs will be much less tired at the end of the day. In actual skiing you don't want to lift that light inside ski up off the snow – it's too much work. Just let the light, inside ski float along on the snow next to the loaded outside ski that's doing all the work. Skiing this way is like walking in slow motion: first one foot...then the other...first one ski...then the other...one complete turn on one foot...then another on the opposite foot....

You'll discover an interesting bonus. Not only are your turns rounder, more carved, more efficient...but your skis will stay closer together. Say goodbye to that old wide track. It's very easy to change the position of the light inside ski in relation to the weighted outside ski. If you stand on both skis equally, trying to move one closer to the other is as impossible as lifting yourself off the ground by your bootstraps.

Nothing else can change your skiing as much as learning to stand exclusively over that outside ski. I call this "the best kept secret in modern skiing" because it's so hard to observe that great skiers are really standing on one foot. But they are, and you can too. Naturally, that's not all there is to polishing your parallel turns, check other Ski Tech sections for more.

PART II   GREATER ASPEN

CHAPTER 3   ASPEN & ITS MOUNTAIN

Aspen is a kind of ultimate, quintessential Colorado ski town in exactly the same way that Vail is a kind of ultimate Colorado ski mountain. Aspen is the one every other ski town gets compared with. The one that's got it all: history and tradition, money and chic, Victorian architecture and post-modern boutiques, culture and clout, narrow streets and tall views, remarkable sophistication, unquenchable enthusiasm. And...oh, yes, good skiing too.

The town of Aspen, like a good-hearted sporting girl from its rowdy mining past, has lived through it all, discovery, abuse and prostitution, good years and bad, has sold or pawned everything it ever held dear, and somehow continues to enchant. For years people have been bemoaning the premature demise of this dynamite town. "Where are all the old locals? Whatever happened to off-season? Remember when Aspen was so small you knew everybody at the post office? The old Aspen we used to know is gone, a victim of its own success, dead..." Believe me, it hasn't happened. Aspen is hipper, trendier, and more expensive than ever. But it's also just as exciting, just as real a place. I'd say that, paradoxically, the secret of Aspen's enduring fascination as a resort is that despite everything it's still more of a community than a resort. Real people, unusual and creative people have put down deep roots here, have made this town different and, in a non-superficial way, more sophisticated than any other ski town, or mountain town in America.

A few years ago I wasn't so crazy about the skiing in Aspen, it was okay, sure, but... That's changed now, with the new gondola and a radical revamping of lifts and services, Aspen Mountain has become one of the best treats advanced skiers can offer themselves. The mountain has always been interesting, but now the bottlenecks and frustrations are gone, and you can ski yourself silly, any day. And that's just on the first of Aspen's four mountains. (We'll visit the other three in the next two chapters). I should quickly add, to set the record straight, that while a week in Aspen is a stunning resort experience for anyone, skiing above town, on Aspen Mountain is not for everyone. This mountain is too hard for a lot of skiers. But Aspen's other three ski mountains (Buttermilk and Aspen Highlands right on the outskirts of town, and Snowmass only a short drive away) take up the slack, offering a wider spectrum of slopes, including fabulous terrain for beginners and novices. All of these mountains are a well integrated part of the Aspen experience. You can have your cake and ski it too, at all four ski areas; or find your own perfect "Aspen area."

I'm lucky in that I get to visit Aspen several times every season. But even though I look forward to skiing on Aspen mountain with something like glee, I look forward even more to just plain being in Aspen. Invariably, when I get home, I remember the conversations, the people I've met, the museum shows and galleries I've taken in, the pulse and panache of Aspen just as vividly as powder mornings on the face of Bell Mountain. You will too.

Because I've promised myself that this book will be, first and foremost, a skier's guide and not a shopping/lodging/dining directory, I want to take you on a guided tour of Aspen mountain, before exploring the town in more detail.

ASPEN'S OWN MOUNTAIN, AN INTRODUCTION

Ajax, which nobody calls Ajax anymore but rather Aspen Mountain, has come a long way since its discovery and launching as a ski area just after World War II. There's an inescapable snob appeal, a built-in cachet to a ski area that doesn't have a single green run! Aspen Mountain deserves it. The skiing is not formidably difficult, it's merely serious – exciting, continuous, sometimes but not always quite challenging. This is skiing for confirmed, even accomplished skiers, not for beginners or novices. Good skiers will find Aspen Mountain as good as they are. And my observation, these last few years, is that there are more strong skiers on this mountain than on any other in Colorado. Not just in numbers; I'm also talking about the average level of skill on these slopes. The *average* skier on Aspen Mountain skis better than the average skier elsewhere in the state.

Aspen Mountain is not a wide ski area, like Vail or Copper or Breckenridge, but instead a long narrow ski area: extending back from the valley floor along the flanks and tops of a couple of long ridges that run down perpendicularly into the Roaring Fork valley. You look up from anywhere in town and the ski mountain looks damn serious, but not very big. Don't be fooled. It goes back, and back, and back. What you see from town is only the tip, or actually the foot, of the iceberg.

Two parallel mountain shapes define this area. On the right side (looking up from town), you'll see the international FIS downhill course peeling down the front face; it drops off a long ridge, which for most of its length is called *Ruthie's Run*, and which runs clear back to the top of the ski mountain. This ridge marks one edge of the ski area. The parallel valley below and east of *Ruthie's* more or less represents the middle of the ski area, and finishes in a classic Aspen run, *Spar Gulch* – the path most skiers take off the mountain. (In the evening, however, *Spar* can be too crowded for comfort, and a last run down *Ruthie's* is a better bet.) The opposite side of *Spar Gulch* is formed by *Bell Mountain*, a second, long, ridge-like shape. *Bell Mountain* has its own mystique and absolutely no easy-angled runs. There are also a number of runs on the far (or eastern) side of *Bell Mountain*, but they all seem to belong to the *Bell Mountain* half of the ski area. These last runs finish in a second rounded gully, *Copper Bowl*. *Copper* is analogous to *Spar Gulch* although less long and wide, and it brings skiers back around the bulk of *Bell Mountain* to join the down-mountain traffic flow in *Spar*.

In short, if you're skiing continuous runs down the mountain, you'll either be skiing somewhere on the *Ruthie's* side, or somewhere on *Bell Mountain* side, or in the valley between them. Simple, right? With this general picture in mind, you can find your way around Aspen Mountain like an old hand. And long continuous runs are definitely what's happening here – a key strategy. But it wasn't always so.

I've already hinted at the major lift changes in recent years which have altered skiing on Aspen Mountain dramatically. But the mega change has been the installation of the Silver Queen gondola, a six passenger beauty that takes skiers from the base to the top of the mountain, a 3,267 vertical-foot hop, in 13 minutes. This lift makes me nostalgic for the Alps because it is of a design seldom seen in America. The Silver Queen was built by the French company, Poma, and the cars are spherical in shape, without doors. Passengers sit back to back and the car hinges apart into two halves when it enters the top or bottom station. French skiers have aptly baptized such gondolas "eggs."

It was obvious from the start that this high-speed, high capacity lift would alter the way people skied on Aspen Mountain. It has, totally. I've spent the most memorable days on this mountain, skiing myself right into the ground, skiing only top-to-bottom runs, and never riding any lift except the gondola. There is a natural tendency, a routine that makes sense at most ski areas, to ride lifts up to the top, and then stay on

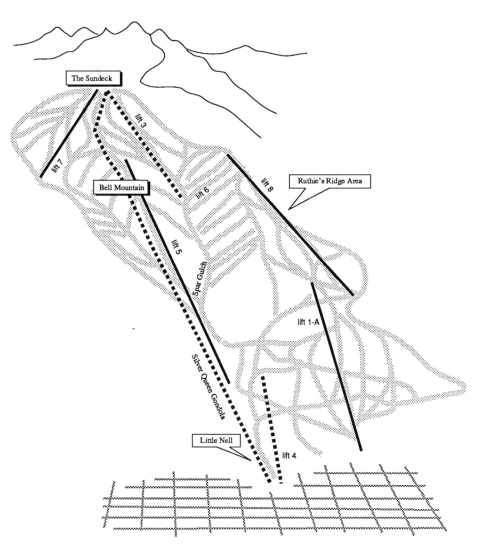

Aspen Mountain—
a sketch map showing
lifts and main runs. For
details, consult the current area trail map
which indicates the names and difficulty of all runs.

the upper slopes all day. This pattern insures that the gondola never seems to get really crowded. It moves so fast that even what looks like a monster line in the morning gets one on board in a few minutes. And finally, even though the very bottom slopes aren't very interesting, strong skiers can shoot across them in a hurry and actually save time by simply skiing down to the bottom every run. This strategy would have been unthinkable a few years ago.

Another dramatic change has occurred in the upper middle mountain with the upgrading of chair 3, now a high-speed detachable quad, that serves the not very steep or difficult central basin above Spar Gulch. This lift, plus the "eggs," has provided a kind of access to Aspen Mountain for skiers who previously wouldn't have dared ski there. It's now possible to ride the Silver Queen to the top, and then just yo-yo around on the easier blue runs served by lift 3, runs like *Pussyfoot*, *Silver Bell*, and *1 & 2 Leaf*, and even take the gondola down in the evening, if you don't feel comfortable on *Spar Gulch*. A lot of weaker skiers have figured this out, which has inevitably led to some serious overcrowding on these easy chair-3 runs.

Why do they bother? Status I guess. It doesn't take long to figure out that Aspen Mountain has the big rep in these parts, is where the heroes ski. And some skiers try to buy in to this mystique before they're ready for it. My recommendation: unless you're truly comfortable on Aspen Mountain (which means, at a minimum, short turns on steeper blue slopes), spend most of your Aspen vacation skiing Snowmass and Buttermilk. No, you certainly won't be bored, and yes, you will make phenomenal progress as a skier. Progress which I guarantee is just about impossible if you start hanging out on Aspen Mountain before you're ready for it. As you'll see in the next two chapters, these other Aspen areas are in no way also-rans or second bests; in many ways they can provide average skiers with a richer, more satisfying experience.

But if you belong on Aspen Mountain, you'll be in hog heaven. And to speed your exploration of this expert's stash, here are a few of my favorite runs.

ASPEN MOUNTAIN, HOT TIPS AND FAVORITE SPOTS

A quality Aspen Mountain experience divides neatly into steep giant-slalom style cruising, and even steeper bump skiing. If you hate moguls, you just won't get all this mountain can offer. But you don't need to spend all day abusing your knees either. One of the big treats here is a "world-class" downhill course – I'm using this much abused adjective literally – which is groomed, maintained and open to regular skiers all season during non-race periods. This run begins at the lower end of *Ruthie's*, and strings together a number of separately named runs, *Aztec*, *Spring Pitch*, *Strawpile*. It's also indicated by "International Downhill" signs and by the fact that these wild big sheets of snow are invariably much smoother than you expect; they are also often bullet-proof from so much preparation. The ski corp (locals still can't get used to calling it the Aspen Skiing Company) grooms these slopes extensively all year long in order to establish a solid base for the annual Aspen Winternational races, a week of World Cup competition when the best international racers slug it out on these slopes.

In fact, you'll find the best non-mogul skiing on, and around, and over toward *Ruthie's* – the lefthand side of the area as you ski down. There are a lot of variations and detours on this big ridge to delight the cruising skier: *Roch Run* and *International* both fit this category, as does *Buckhorn*, the best way to start in this direction off the top.

A quick glance at the trail map shows you that there are still three marked levels of difficulty on this mountain: green runs are missing, but double black diamonds have been added at the top of the scale. Any-thing marked double-black is not merely steep and moguled; but the moguls themselves will be of the extra-demanding rather than garden-variety sort. Let's start with some friendlier bumpy lines:

First off, the *Face of Bell Mountain*. This is a beaut. Ski down *1 & 2 Leaf* and cut left just under the top of Bell Mountain, traversing out on its flank to arrive at the first of a series of open moguled faces, separated by long hedgerow lines of evergreens. Bumps on the *Face of Bell* are usually large and round with more than enough space beneath each one to complete your turn and control your speed. Welcoming, enticing bumps. There's a special way to ski the *Face of Bell*: start anywhere, ski most of the way down, but before you actually reach *Spar Gulch* turn right in a long horizontal traverse which will take you across to the next open face. Locals refer to this as "going back up." Since *Spar Gulch* (which is the "floor" beneath the *Face of Bell*) keeps dropping away, each traverse brings you "back up" to the top of another bump slope. You can repeat the process again and again for one of the most satisfy-ing bump runs around.

Bell mountain has other less-than-fierce bump lines to check out on its far, eastern side: *Christmas Tree*, and a generalized area called *Back of Bell*. But on this side the trees are denser, the openings smaller; and although the bumps are still smooth and friendly, there is less space to navigate in. Very quickly you'll find that this mountain pushes you onto steeper, more challenging, double black runs. It's not the steepness that creates the difficulty, but usually the fact that the bumps are tighter, less rhythmic, and the gullies between them sharper and narrower. This gives you less space to finish turns and slow down – fewer choices. Even so, Aspen's most difficult bumps are merely tight, not ugly – probably because the technical level of the skiers making them is higher than that at many other resorts. For experts in search of a workout, the *Ridge of Bell*, a long steep nose facing straight down toward Aspen offers the most the challenging skiing on this side of the mountain.

There are a lot of exciting double-black gullies, steep and rather narrow, on the front face above town. But there's not always enough snow this low on the mountain to cover all the rocks on such steep slopes, so I only ski these runs on really big snow years. *Corkscrew* and *Corkscrew Gully* are the best of these lower bump slots.

Aspen's toughest bump runs are found in two separate zones: the *mine dumps* and *Walsh's*. The mine dumps are a series of thrilling, half-open gashes through the steep aspen forest on the west bank of Spar Gulch – *Bear Paw* through *Last Dollar*. The dumps were originally created when miners pushed the slag and rubble from their "holes" down the mountainside. Unless you can successfully launch a turn, any time, on any bump, no matter how weird, don't tempt fate over here.... Try to ski the mine dumps early in the morning, they catch the first sun beautifully.

Walsh's Gulch used to be the most infamous out-of-bounds skiing at Aspen (along with nearby *Difficult Gulch* which is still out of bounds). These two renegade powder paths lead down steep, cliff-cut slopes into the Roaring Fork valley miles upstream from Aspen; and over the years they have claimed a respectable number of avalanche victims. The ski area has now controlled and opened the best of it, the upper slopes of *Walsh's* and a couple of parallel lines next door, *Hyrup's* and *Kristi*. These are short but fierce runs, steep enough to make even brilliant skiers "pay attention." A must if you want to have skied the most serious slopes on the mountain.

But don't make the mistake of taking chair 7 back to the top when you come out of *Walsh's*. This must be the world's slowest quad, and it spoils a thrilling run with a boring aftermath. Better to head on down the eastern border of the ski area and enjoy the most obscure skiing on Aspen mountain: *Gentleman's Ridge* and the gladed trees below it (*Jackpot*, just below *Gentleman's Ridge*, used to be out of bounds). These runs are so far off the beaten path they don't see much traffic, but they don't get groomed either which means more bumps. They also catch the afternoon sun so there's no hurry to get there early.

Actually, given the number of bumps, Aspen mountain is not the greatest powder skiing venue, even after a serious dump. The very best powder skiing in these parts, period, is that offered by the snow-cat powder tours on the backside of Aspen Mountain. This is an all-day adventure (with lunch) where you'll ski magnificent open slopes in what was once to have been the "Little Annie" ski area, in the company of experienced powder guides. These tours are run by the Aspen Skiing Company; and considering the quality of the skiing, are very affordable. Sign up early, at the offices below the gondola.

LUNCH TIME

Lunch, on mountain and off, is better around Aspen than in most ski resorts. For one thing, in a move as clever as it is rare, the "ski corp" doesn't operate the on-mountain eateries but leases them to individual owner/operators who compete fiercely, and add a refreshing individuality to each one. This is true at all three of the mountains run by the Aspen Skiing Company, Aspen Mountain, Buttermilk and Snowmass; and skiers benefit enormously. One wonders how long such enlightenment can last if corporate bean-counters ever really start trying to maximize their profits. Aspen Mountain has three lunch spots: The Sundeck on top offers better views than food, but the view off the backside of the mountain into the heart of the Elk range with 14,000-foot summits lined up like special effects for a Spielberg film, is quite enough. Bonnie's at Tourtelotte Park serves a legendary Apple Strudel, and it's often argued that a trip to Aspen is wasted unless you sample this Bavarian classic. A newer restaurant complex, Ruthie's, near the bottom of *Ruthie's Run* between lifts 1-A and 8, features a restaurant-within-a-restaurant, Darcy's, for sit-down lunches. The in-town options are obvious, since the Gondola tends to lure good skiers to the bottom so often. My own favorite Aspen lunch spot is Poppycock's, a knockout bistro only two blocks from the gondola building.

ASPEN AMBIANCE, ASPEN STYLE

Did I talk about skiing yourself silly? The Silver Queen gondola gives you so much vertical so quickly that you can really hurt yourself. Lots of skiers, strong skiers, hang it up before the lifts close because their legs are saying: please! In Aspen it's okay to quit early, there's enough to do off the slopes.

For years and years, Aspen *apres* has begun, regular as ritual, at Little Nell's, the funky, old-fashioned, rundown, crowded, wonderful slope-side bar at the bottom of *Little Nell*, the last and lowest slope into town below *Spar Gulch.* But Little Nell's is dead, long live Little Nell's! The bar was sacrificed on the altar of a massive base redevelopment project, and a new, slicker Little Nell's built in its place. The jury's still out. Only time will tell where the ski patrollers and instructors, debutantes and demi monde will wind up. There will always be a number one locals' apres-ski bar, but I'll leave finding the next one up the reader as an exercise....

Not classic apres ski, but my own favorite after a hard day on Aspen mountain is cappuccino at the upstairs cafe in the Explore Bookstore across from the Jerome Hotel – an Aspen treasure, this wonderful Victorian house/bookstore/cafe is one of the last things you'd ever expect to find at a ski resort. But then Aspen is different.

It's the most complex, intriguing and hard-to-pin-down ski town I know: arty, design-conscious, too sophisticated for its Levis britches and still just right. If Vail represents *nouveau riche* ski society, then Aspen could be characterized as *old-money.* (Like Vail, but in a completely different way, Aspen is a great vacation spot even if you don't ski.) Aspen's real secret isn't money at all, but the large underground of writers, artists and other creative refugees from the so-called real world who have gravitated to the Roaring Fork Valley over the last thirty years – and have given this town an unexpected, disarming sophistication. Aspen's sophistication somehow transcends, the normal ski-world reality of development pressures, scheming real-estate villains and tourist-dollar feeding frenzies that all successful ski resorts fall prey to. Even the newly arrived visitor, who obviously doesn't have a circle of fascinating Aspen fringe types and friends, can feel this sophistication in the streets. Galleries here show serious art not just fun prints; Aspen fashions are real fashions, not just fun furs. Aspen Magazine is the most polished and ambitious resort magazine in the country, showcasing writing and cultural reporting you'd expect to find in New York, LA or Santa Fe – because the Aspen public, local and transient is tuned into the arts in a way that no other ski town can imagine much less equal.

No other ski town has anything like the Aspen Museum of Art. It's an old brick power house transformed into a post-modern palazzo just across the Roaring Fork River, a few blocks from downtown. Shows here generally tour LA, Chicago and New York museums. A must visit if you're into contemporary art. Shopping as art, albeit wacky pop art, got a curious boost with the opening of Boogies Diner, a two-story pastiche of avant garde and retro trends and trendiness. Some Aspenites swore it was the end of the world, but I guess they had no sense of humor.

And eating out.... There is too much choice, too many good choices for serious reviewing in this short a chapter. Suffice it to say that you can find almost anything, and spend any sized fortune in Aspen's restaurants. If money is no object, the most creative cooking in town is found at Gordons; but unless you're a celebrity you run the chance of being neglected or abused. More congenial and in the same culinary league is Piñons. One restaurant where you won't spend a fortune, intimate and unpretentious – and delicious too – is Cache Cache, run by a delightful and forever overworked young French couple, who also recently opened Café Bonjour next door.

Where is next door? How do you find things, places, addresses in Aspen? Although Aspen is the largest "ski town" in Colorado, its downtown core is compact and intimate. Two one block long pedestrian malls define the center of the grid; and when you ask directions, the reply will probably be in terms of a number of blocks north or south or up or down from the mall. Still the malls are the little that came late. Aspen doesn't function as a real pedestrian village and parking is a nightmare. In-town ransportation is a little awkward; and the buses between ski areas are far more convenient than anything within Aspen. An unsolved problem. Still, once you're downtown you can walk everywhere.

So naturally the two hotels I'm going to recommend are within walking distance of everything. Recommend? Well, not for everyone, because both the Jerome Hotel and the Hotel Lenado are rather expensive, actually very expensive; but they're also very wonderful. The Jerome is Aspen's pearl: a classic historical structure from the glory days of Aspen silver mining, it has just undergone a major restoration, and the new addition behind the hotel surprised almost everybody – it's a perfect complement to the old grande dame of a hotel. A classic. If you can't afford to stay at the Jerome, as most of us can't, at least raise a glass in its bar. The Hotel Lenado, diagonally across from Paepcke Park, is a different story altogether. A modern pocket hotel designed by Aspen architectural wizard, Harry Teague, the Lenado is an intimate, low-key, post-modern masterpiece in pale wood and Buddhist prayer-flag colors. It's the best new hotel in the Rockies. Of course, Aspen has the whole spectrum of skier accommodations, but these two come close to some Platonic ideal of perfect ski resort lodging.

What more can I add except: enjoy. At the end of a week-long stay, you'll have the impression that you're just beginning to get the hang of this remarkable ski town. It's the beginning of an addiction.

ASPEN DATA

KEY PHONE NUMBERS

Snow Conditions	(303) 925-1221
Area Information	1-800-525-6200
Central Reservations	1-800-525-6200

TRANSPORTATION

By car, 4 1/2 hour drive from Denver on I-70 to Glenwood Springs and then south on Highway 82 (in good road and weather conditions).

By bus or limo, or High Mountain Taxi (vans) from Denver's Stapleton Airport.

By plane, via Continental Express or United Express from Denver's Stapleton Airport to Aspen. Also non-stop jet flights from several major cities.

MOUNTAIN STATISTICS

Vertical Drop	3,267 feet
Base Elevation	7,945 feet
Summit Elev.	11,212 feet
Skiing Terrain	625 acres
Longest Run	3 miles
Number of Lifts	8 including, 1 high-speed detachable quad and one gondola
Uphill Capacity	10,775 skiers per hour
Snowboarding	no!

Aspen lift tickets are good at Snowmass and Buttermilk. A ticket good at all 4 Aspen areas can also be purchased.

What keeps some skiers off steep slopes, while others can't get enough steep black skiing? The difference is short turns – not just short, but smoothly, crisply linked short turns, right down the fall line, tick-tock, side-to-side, as inevitable and rhythmic as a pendulum. Short swing, as it's often called, is the key that unlocks steep, narrow and challenging terrain. (Medium and long turns build up too much speed, too fast.) And as usual, there's a trick to it. I call this trick, or technique, dynamic anticipation. *It works like this:*

Suppose, before turning your skis down the hill, your whole upper body – hips, shoulders, head and arms – was already turned, aimed down the hill. Then your skis would turn faster and easier, pivoting rapidly around to line up beneath your body which was already in the fall line. *Less mass (less stuff) to turn means less effort needed, which in turn means faster, snappier results – the very essence of short linked turns. In skiing this pre-twisting of the upper body in the direction of the coming turn has always been called* anticipation. *But we can do better.*

Our goal is not to turn the body first and then let the skis catch up, but instead to let our bodies move straight down the slope while legs and skis pivot back and forth beneath us. That's where the action is, down below the stable quiet mass of the upper body. And it's this back and forth, windup and release, pre-turn and re-turn sort of action that I call dynamic anticipation. *Everyone has seen and admired this type of skiing, but how do you learn it?*

It isn't so very easy. Dynamic anticipation is the watershed skill that divides average good skiers from extremely good skiers. But here's a simple game plan:

First, be sure you're skiing in a loose upright stance with a very relaxed lower back. This is the region that acts as a pivot point or hinge letting legs and skis turn beneath you without the body itself turning. If you're bent forward with a hollow, tight lower back, nothing will work.

Next, try a few hockey stops. Slide straight down the hill and twist your legs and skis sideways to a stop beneath you. They turn, you don't. After you get the hang of it, smooth your hockey stops out into round uphill curves that work the same way: skis turning up the hill but body floating along motionless above them, still facing down the fall line. We call these uphill curves with anticipation (that uninvolved, motionless upper body) preturns.

The preturn—first by itself and then used to launch a turn.

Then use your preturns to launch new turns down the hill. Just add a pole plant while shifting your weight to the top ski and, wham, the skis will (or should) turn back downhill almost on their own. That's the reaction from the action of the pre turn. And of course, you'll want to capture this feeling, prolong it in a continuous series of turns, the end of each turn becoming the preturn, or wind up, for the next turn.

Short turns: quiet body, active legs.

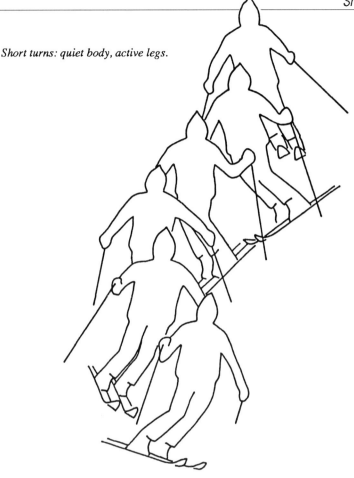

What I've just given you is only the bare outline of a game plan to develop dynamic anticipation (for the details see Chapter 4 of my book, Breakthrough on Skis) but it should give you a sense of what's involved in developing short turns. The more natural your anticipation becomes, that is, the more your upper body relaxes and floats instead of actively turning from side to side with your skis, the easier you will find it to link short turns.

One last tip. The trigger, the signal that launches one turn right after another down the fall line is always a pole plant. By reaching straight down the hill with your pole, rather than letting it swing around and across the hill with your skis, you will be helping to keep your body lined up in that going-down-the-mountain direction. Short turns in a nutshell: you keep going straight down the mountain while your skis twist back and forth beneath you.

CHAPTER 4   NEAR ASPEN

The two ski areas we're going to visit in this chapter, Buttermilk and Aspen Highlands, don't exactly loom up dramatically over town — but almost. It wouldn't be an exaggeration, considering how Aspen has grown, to say that these two areas are in the suburbs, or outskirts of Aspen. Close enough to belong. And more important, different enough from Aspen Mountain itself to balance out the town's ski offering .

Skiing at Buttermilk, or to give it its whole name, Buttermilk-Tiehack, is doubtless the most under-rated ski experience in Aspen. I really like this little mountain. A lot of skiers write Buttermilk off as Aspen's beginner area. But it's a lot more than that. Sure Buttermilk skiing is pretty easy for the most part, no heroes no hotdoggers, *ni trompettes ni tambours*, no guts or glory associated with skiing on this mountain. But what about charm? The runs are beautifully cut. The terrain is mostly low-angle but has lots of variation, lots of character. You'll find extremely esthetic upper intermediate runs on the Tiehack side of this mountain. And yes, it is a great place for beginners, as well as a wide range of learning skiers. I'm hoping that after reading my review of Buttermilk you won't underestimate it either.

Aspen Highlands, I regret to say, is a bit over-rated; and doesn't compete strongly with the three other Aspen ski mountains. Believe me, I would rather be singing its praises, because Highlands is a kind of maverick ski area, run by a separate company and not a part of the Aspen Skiing Company's seamless corporate world, and I love mavericks. But it's not a natural ski mountain, and its lift layout and skier services seem antiquated in comparison with Aspen's other mountains. Highlands has stood still in time, while the white revolution has transformed skiing all around it.

Does this mean that you shouldn't ski Highlands during your Aspen sojourn. Not at all, but I don't recommend spending most of your week there. A day, two days maximum. It's always a treat to ski new slopes, anywhere, and there are a few special Highlands' experiences that I'll spotlight for you. With all it's old-fashioned quirkiness Highlands can add interesting variety to your Aspen ski vacation. But now, let's zoom in on suburban Aspen skiing:

BUTTERMILK, THE BIGGEST LITTLE AREA IN ASPEN

Buttermilk-Tiehack is an easy mountain to understand; it's a three pronged area, with three major branch-like skiing zones slanting down from its summit ridge. The front side, or Main Buttermilk, is a tongue of interlaced blue and green runs served by two chairs, that drops straight down, northward, toward the main base. Another branch of the area is Tiehack, slanting down to the east (in the direction of town). Tiehack, with one long chairlift back to the top and a short one to nowhere right at the bottom, is considerably steeper and full of blue and blue/black runs. And finally, slanting down diagonally to the other side you have West Buttermilk, another gentle area of blue and green runs, but for me more esthetic skiing than that on the front side with longer, more sweeping downvalley views. (Both the western and eastern branches of Buttermilk, Tiehack and West Buttermilk, have their own bases with small parking lots.)

West Buttermilk also has another plus, Cafe Suzanne. Cafe Suzanne at the base of the West Buttermilk lift is not the ritziest mountain restaurant at an Aspen ski area, it doesn't have the biggest menu, nor the best food – that honor probably goes to Gwyn's restaurant at Snowmass. But this one's my favorite. Witty and unpretentious, Cafe Suzanne serves yummy crepes for lunch and momentarily makes you feel you're in a hut, not a restaurant, somewhere in the Alps. Then the West Buttermilk lift, chair 3, takes you back up to a slightly higher summit. From here you can begin one of the loveliest runs at the area, a ridge run, all the way down to the bottom of Tiehack via *Tom's Thumb*, *Tiehack Parkway* and *Racer's Edge*. This edge of the ski area is particularly impressive because it overlooks Maroon Creek, the deep alpine valley separating Buttermilk from Highlands. The view from the Cliff House terrace out over this valley is one of the grandest at Aspen.

As a beginner, novice and low intermediate area, Buttermilk works exactly as you would expect it to. The green runs are an honest green; you can't get in trouble here, you can't get lost. If you're a beginner or novice skier at Aspen, looking for lessons, but you don't want to go all the way out to Snowmass every day – where you'll also find superb learning terrain – this is the place! In addition to regular ski school here,

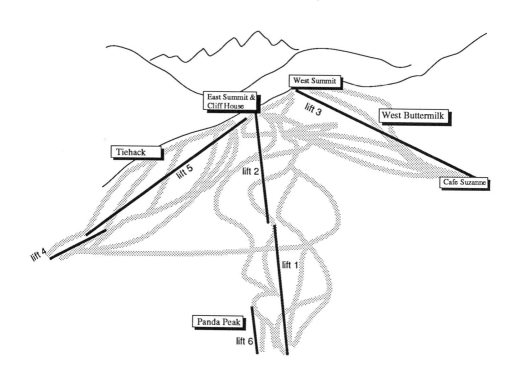

Buttermilk—
a sketch map showing
lifts and main runs. For
details, consult the current area trail map
which indicates the names and difficulty of all runs.

Buttermilk is home of the Powder Pandas, a day care/skiing program for mini ski visitors, 3 to 6 years old.

It doesn't surprise anyone when I say that Buttermilk has lots of inviting, gentle terrain for new and weaker skiers; that's been its reputation from the beginning. What really does surprise people is that Buttermilk is such a enjoyable mountain for better skiers. This has nothing to do with the difficulty or challenge of the skiing, even on the more serious Tiehack side. The pleasure comes from the unusually open character of the runs. Buttermilk runs are just that, real runs rather than mere "trails" or slots cut through forest. Buttermilk's runs seem to have been there from the beginning, as natural open glades. That is not really the case, this mountain was cut for skiing. But the feel of these wide, free-form, non-trails is just right: an invitation to swoop, to move around and fill up space with long traverses and curves rather than heading right down the groove in a businesslike, no-nonsense way. I really like this sort of skiing.

Of course, Buttermilk just isn't big enough or varied enough to keep good skiers stimulated day after day. Like Highlands, this is not a place to spend a whole week, but give it at least a day! A parenthesis in time, a vacation from the bigger-is-better school of thought that all serious skiers fall into. A vacation that substitutes relaxation and humor for challenge. Just below the get-on ramp for lift 2 on Main Buttermilk is a wonderful sign: *"The Wall of Death, the World's Shortest Black Run."* It's true, three moguls worth. And further down the front, small trails for kids go snaking off into the forest with names like, *The Black Hole*, tacked up on spontaneous looking, child-sized trail signs in the middle of the forest. Buttermilk at its best reminds us that skiing is not so all-fired serious.

TIEHACK

What does such a droll word mean? It refers to trees cut expressly to make cross ties for early railroad beds; by extension a "tiehack" is a stand of forest where these ties were cut. Now you know. Did you also know that Tiehack, the eastern side of Buttermilk, is one of the better spots at Aspen to ski powder after a big dump? So few skiers head over to this "unfashionable" mountain that powder lasts a good deal longer here than on Aspen Mountain. And Tiehack is so compact, served by one main lift, that you don't waste a lot of time getting to your powder slopes or traversing back from them either. The slopes here are wide and undulating, respectably inclined but never steep enough to give you pause. At many areas these black slopes would legitimately be marked blue. This is not expert but only upper-intermediate skiing, yet bloody good upper-intermediate skiing. Tiehack has become an active ski racing site in recent times; there are new electronic timing facilities here for NASTAR and self-timer courses, and lots of junior and amateur races are run here. There's a natural giant-slalom flavor about this terrain that makes you ski it in big fast turns as well, even if you haven't worn a racing bib for years.

Tiehack is also what makes Buttermilk into a fine all-around learning mountain as well as just a beginner/novice mountain. The most interesting instruction program in the Aspen area takes place here: the

Vic Braden Ski College, an intensive week-long saturation ski program, designed to push weaker skiers into and right through the intermediate ranks. I haven't yet had the pleasure of personally observing a full week of the ski college in action, but I have heard a number of rave reviews from students who've gone through the course. And I can tell you that the general approach is right on. An intensive, continuous period of instruction/learning/practice with video feedback built into the program is the best way to stage a breakthrough in your skiing performance. A couple of hours of lessons, a half day, a day, or even a lot of occasional lessons spaced out over the course of a season just don't add up to significant changes in skiing performance – at least not for the vast majority of skiers. The Vic Braden Ski College is pimarily a program aimed at weak skiers who want to become strong intermediates, but I can tell you that the same approach would work wonders for intermediates who are serious about breaking into expert skiing.

My experience directing a similar, week-long intensive program, the Ski Clinic at Squaw Valley, convinced me that this much time and concentration, in this sort of a focused setting, is an optimum recipe for dramatic progress. Vic Braden, of course, is known as a tennis coach not a skiing guru, but in fact, his role in the program has been more the creation of an optimized context in which gifted instructors and motivated students can spend enough time together to make a difference. A most interesting program. I wish there were more programs like this in American skiing. And with Tiehack extending the range of its practice terrain, Buttermilk is a good home for it.

ASPEN HIGHLANDS, THE MAVERICK

Nature hasn't exactly favored Highlands, except perhaps in terms of spectacular views. It's a difficult mountain to ski well, or to serve well. Like Aspen Mountain, Highlands is a long thin area extending back from the base on a north-south axis. But where Aspen Mountain has both ridges and valleys for a pleasing variety of terrain, Aspen Highlands is really only one long ridge – a crest from which the terrain drops off steeply on both sides. This means that there's a serious lack of natural fall-line skiing. Straight descents to one side or the other of the central ridge line always exact a toll in tiresome come-back traverses. And even though its brochures boast of the longest vertical drop in Colorado, some 3,800 vertical feet, Highlands doesn't have as much ski terrain as that would suggest because, of necessity, most runs are crowded in close to the crest of this long ridge.

It's a great game at Rocky Mountain ski resorts to try to second guess the area's designers and say: "I would have done it this way, I would have put this lift there, cut that run the other way...." But frankly, I don't know what they could have done differently here. It's just a tough hill on which to create a satisfying ski area. Let me instead start with a catalog of things they've done well.

For years Highlands has welcomed freestyle skiers and "alternative" sliders of all sorts with open arms. Every Friday for years they've hosted a freestyle/bump contest. And their ski school even offers a "Change of Pace Clinic" – name your weapons: snowboard, monoski or telemark. Bravo! I love this sort of open-mindedness. They have also marked their runs accurately and honestly. This is rarer than you might think. Often areas that don't have much hard skiing jack up the ratings to make their trail maps look a little more serious. And other ski areas that are shy on good intermediate terrain, consistently under-rate the difficulty of their runs, to make average skiers think they have more terrain to play on than they really do. Not Highlands. Here the double diamond runs on *Steeplechase* and *Olympic Bowl* are legitimate experts-only terrain. The blacks are honestly hard, and so on.

How does this mountain work? Right at the base there is a large open bowl, *Powder Bowl*, facing somewhat west – a real visual land-mark, that looks more inviting than it actually is, because the sun hammers the snow on this exposure, especially in spring, and despite its name powder doesn't stay powder here for long. But Powder Bowl is a kind of detour; the main route up the mountain starts with lift 1, a diagonal access chair rising through steep forests. Chair 2, right in line, takes you further up the ridge and serves an area of very easy skiing. Chair 2 is the novice, low-intermediate zone for Highlands. Inexperienced skiers can spend most of their day up here, eat at the mid-mountain restaurant on top of lift 2, and then come back to the base via *Park Avenue*, the only easy trail down from the middle mountain. Unless you're a pretty secure parallel skier I wouldn't recommend venturing above the Merry Go Round restaurant at the top of lift 2; there just isn't any more easy skiing up there.

There is, on the contrary quite a bit of steep and challenging skiing at the uppermost end of Highlands' long ridge, or more accurately, on either side of its upper ridge. To reach the top from the Merry Go Round restaurant, you still have to take some combination of lifts 3, 4 and 5 and when they get there, good skiers have two stimulating choices. On the eastern side is a zone of small steep faces known collectively as *Steeplechase* – from top to bottom: *Kessler Bowl, Snyder's Ridge, Sodd Buster, Garmisch* and *St. Moritz. Kessler Bowl* is just open enough to

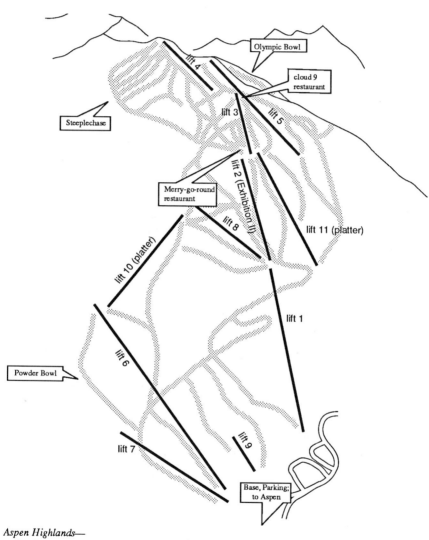

Aspen Highlands—
a sketch map
showing lifts and main runs.
For details, consult the
current area trail map which
indicates the names and difficulty of all runs.

almost deserve its name and looks like the best skiing up here; but it's been closed for one reason or another every time I've skied Highlands, so that's just a guess. The others are all fiery bump pitches; their top-of-the-mountain location guarantees the sort of cold, dry, firm snow that makes steep skiing a pleasure; and they all get lovely morning light. *Steeplechase* is exciting enough to ski, but the long and boring traverse back to the center of the mountain, and the complex chair hopping to get back to the top dampen one's enthusiasm for repeating the experience.

On the other side of the summit ridge is a pitch that gets my adrenalin pumping a lot harder than *Steeplechase*. That's *Olympic Bowl*, which isn't a bowl at all, no matter what the PR guys say, but instead is a very steep and exposed bump face. The views here, across steep and wild out-of-bounds country toward Pyramid Peak, are as dramatic as you can find at Aspen. And this run is steep enough that a fall would be terribly unpleasant. For good skiers in search of excitement. The *Glades* next door to *Olympic Bowl* are a little more forgiving, a lot more varied, and have the advantage of a shorter come back traverse to the base of lift 5. In general I think you're better off to cut right, back to lift 5, at the base of all of these "Olympic area" runs rather than continuing on down the flank of the mountain via *Robinson's Run*, which is narrow and uninviting and will cost you a long poma-lift ride back up to the base of lift 3.

There's the rub. For all the good skiing on this mountain, you have to constantly plan your strategy to avoid winding up miles from nowhere. One could deal with all this a little more easily if the lifts were faster. But the white revolution in ski lifts hasn't reached Aspen Highlands. In many ways this area is frozen in time. Old Riblet double chairs are the norm. The two platter pulls don't serve the "new" function of opening up high, alpine terrain the way they do at Copper Mountain or Crested Butte, but seem to be left-over, stop-gap measures from an earlier era. The mountain signage is small, old fashioned and hard to read. And the ski school here is the last surviving hold-out in Colorado of Cliff Taylor's direct parallel, or GLM method, that starts folks out on three-foot mini skis. This is a method that was conceived decades ago in response to the extreme difficulty of turning long stiff skis. Such a method is no longer needed with softer modern skis, and actually cheats skiers out of the skills they need to make a modern ski work for them. *Caveat aprentor!*

One old-time tradition at Highlands that I can really applaud, however, is the classic Ski Patrol jump over the deck of the Cloud 9 restaurant near the top of lift 3. This is a real show that takes place around noon several times a week, and features patrol members flying off an enormous Gelände kicker that launches them clear across the deck of the restaurant onto a steep landing below. The show's finale usually involves a patroller pulling a rescue toboggan after him through the air, and leaves onlookers speechless. If the weather's good, which it has to be for the jump to take place, stick around for lunch at the outdoor grill. The Cloud 9 deck has the same outrageous view of Pyramid Peak that makes *Olympic Bowl* so special.

And before we leave Highlands, a couple of final tips: The runs on chair 3 are certainly the most "conventional" in the sense that they are direct, no-nonsense fall-line runs, with no long traverses. This is a dense zone of good upper intermediate skiing, where you can make a lot of turns in a short time with no long lift lines and no frustrations. And on the way down the mountain, strong skiers should be sure to check out *Bob's Glades* – my own favorite run at Highlands – seldom packed out, never bumped out. This is a wonderful slope of wide-open trees near lift 8 which gets very little traffic and after a good storm is the most intriguing powder skiing at Highlands. Although marked double diamond, it is nowhere near as steep as *Steeplechase* or *Olympic Bowl*, and there's plenty of room to maneuver between the trees. A gem.

BUTTERMILK DATA

MOUNTAIN STATISTICS

Vertical Drop	2,030 feet
Summit Elev.	9,800 feet
Base Elevation	7,770 feet
Skiing Terrain	410 acres
Number of Lifts	6 including one platter pull
Uphill Capacity	6,297 skiers per hour
Snowboarding	Yes
Transportation	Free shuttle bus from downtown Aspen
Tickets	Buttermilk tickets are good at Aspen Mountain & Snowmass; tickets good at all 4 Aspen areas available.
Phone Numbers	See Aspen Data page

ASPEN HIGHLANDS DATA

KEY PHONE NUMBERS

Snow Conditions	(303) 925-5300
Area Information	(303) 925-5300

MOUNTAIN STATISTICS

Vertical Drop	3,800 feet
Summit Elev.	11,800 feet
Base Elevation	8000 feet
Skiing Terrain	540 acres
Longest Run	3 1/2 miles
Number of Lifts	11 including 2 platter pull lifts
Uphill Capacity	10,000 skiers per hour
Snowboarding	Yes
Transportation	Free shuttle bus from downtown Aspen
Tickets	A ticket good at all 4 Aspen areas can also be purchased.

SKI TECH: STRATEGIES FOR LEARNING

There's no way to become an accomplished skier without paying your dues. Frustration, falls, occasional failure and lots of days, lots of miles on skis are part of the recipe. But there are also short cuts, learning strategies that will make your practice time pass more quickly, will get you where you want to go faster. Here's my list of suggestions for faster, more efficient progress.

Terrain will be your best teacher. It's humbling for a ski instructor like myself to admit this, but it's true. You should learn to distinguish between three types of ski terrain: practice/learning slopes, pleasure/ performance slopes, and challenging slopes. Basically "learning terrain" is ski terrain that's a little too easy for you. Slopes so easy there is absolutely no doubt in your mind that you can make every mistake in the book and still recover. This is essential if you are going to concentrate 100% on new, hence psychologically risky moves. It's even true in bumps. You will master medium-size bumps by practicing in trivial mini-bumps, learn to ski giant man-eating moguls by practicing the moves in comfy medium-sized ones. Always pick practice/learning terrain that's too easy; it frees your mind.

At the other end of the scale you'll find "adventure" or "challenge" terrain: slopes that are honestly too hard, where you're scrambling just to survive. It's okay to ski over your head from time to time, and can be a confidence builder of a sort. But don't let friends, or your own ego, push you over your head too often. It will permanently retard your progress as a skier by reinforcing awkward survival moves to the point of ingrained habits. Your best bet for rapid progress is to spend about two-thirds to three-quarters of your skiing day on performance slopes (slopes in your comfort range) and the rest of the time really concentrating on repeating key moves on easier "learning terrain." But don't practice anything all day long, or even for hours on end; you'll burn out. Better to ski three runs for the hell of it, and then slow down and focus your attention on skiing form for just one good run. A good instructor will automatically strive for this sort of balance between concentrated focused practice and relaxed pleasure skiing where you can slowly "ski in" the new habits.

But while constant attempts to practice new skiing skills, hour after hour, are usually counter-productive, it is still a good idea to devote a week of time to achieving some sort of major goal, a breakthrough in your skiing. Whether a simple week of group lessons, or a more focused program like the Vic Braden Ski College I mentioned in the last chapter, the effect of such commitment is cumulative and dramatic. On the other hand, one or two hour lessons are a waste of time for most skiers. And half-day lessons or three-hour "clinics" are about as successful as any other quick-fix remedies, i.e. not effective at all in terms of changing your basic skiing habits. It takes time. And the advantage of longer lessons (all day at a minimum, or week-long if possible) is that your instructor will have sufficient time to guide and adjust the alternation of focused practice periods with spontaneous skiing mileage in such a way as to achieve the greatest results, and the longest lasting ones.

Finally, focus on one thing, one movement, one skill, one skiing pattern at a time. No one can do more. Don't let your concentration get fragmented by half a dozen well intentioned tips. A good instructor may express the same point in a variety of ways, but he or she will continue to guide you toward one goal at a time. For example to master modern parallel skiing you will need to master both one-footed balance on the outside ski, and early weight transfer at the start of your turn. But you can't do both at once. Master first one, then the other.

CHAPTER 5   SNOWMASS

I can't talk about Snowmass without making someone mad at me. But I better tell it like it is: Snowmass is hands down the best all-round ski area in Aspen, yet it's nonetheless only *a part* of Aspen. If Snowmass were somewhere else, all by itself, it would still be one of the big three in Colorado, along with Vail and Steamboat. In fact, Snowmass has been working at developing an independent resort identity ever since its first lifts opened – trying to persuade guests to love it for itself, as Snowmass, not as part of greater Aspen – but it hasn't really worked.

Yes, there is a village up there, in a lovely broad side valley above the Roaring Fork, only 20 minutes drive from Aspen. There's an amazing variety of attractive condominium lodging in Snowmass too. Snowmass is a fine place to stay not just to ski, especially with a family, but…. The "but" in this case is that beds alone don't make a resort, much less a ski town. Snowmass Mall, the central plaza, which is the shopping area and heart of this resort, is little more than a block long. Even with the recent addition of about thirty new commercial spaces and a couple of restaurants (which doubles the retail space in the Snowmass core) one modest mall and a big convention center simply don't add up to an exciting ski town. As soon as they've kicked off their ski boots, savvy Snowmass skiers head for Aspen.

But as a mountain, I give Snowmass only rave reviews. You will too. I've never stayed at Snowmass, but I've found it to be a pretty effortless trip up from Aspen, either by the free shuttle bus, or in your own car, so there's no reason for any visitors, anywhere in the Aspen area, not to ski Snowmass to their hearts' content. Like Vail, it's an all-around mountain for every member of the family, every skill level, with separate zones that feel like separate ski mountains in their own right. And like other Aspen Skiing Company mountains, the level of skier service at Snowmass is very slick, polished and gracious. The white revolution has transformed this mountain which, today, is an absolute bargain for your lift dollar.

THE SHAPE AND FEEL OF THE MOUNTAIN.

Wide open spaces – that's how I'd start out, telling a friend about Snowmass. The most celebrated ski terrain here is the *Big Burn*, a large mountainside, half denuded of trees by an ancient fire. While the *Big Burn* is only a tiny section of modern Snowmass, it is still an effective symbol of the flavor and feel of this mountain – room to move.

Snowmass is a very wide, spread-out mountain, and the only problem with having so much room to move is that, without a clear mental picture of the whole area, you can wind up wasting a lot of time just getting from one place to another. (Trail condition reports at the bottom of lifts make your early morning decisions about where to ski easier.) For example, if you're skiing in the higher zones, it isn't a good idea to ski back to the village for lunch. And if you start your skiing day on one side of the mountain and discover that you really want to be on the other side, it may take you a couple of hours to get there. This is not a disadvantage, just a fact of life on a really big ski mountain. And Snowmass is that. So I'll try to paint a quick picture of how the mountain is laid out and then offer some strategies for different levels of skiers, in search of differing experiences on this friendly giant.

Snowmass divides, more or less naturally, into five different skiing areas. Look straight uphill from Snowmass Village and you'll see the lifts and runs of *Sam's Knob*, not too poetic a name but an apt one for what is essentially just a bump on a long high ridge. This is a high traffic area, full of skiers heading out into the back of the Snowmass beyond. But thanks to a couple of high-speed quads, it's not a bottleneck. The upper slopes of *Sam's Knob* are wide blue freeways. The very bottom part of this front hillside turns into *Fanny Hill*, a gentle beginners area that laps up against Snowmass Village. The staggered tiers of lodging units rising uphill past the village core provide the most convenient ski-in, ski-out situation you'll find anywhere in Colorado. I should also tell you that the new restaurant on top of *Sam's Knob*, Ce Ce's, has the best views on the mountain – you eat looking directly out over the bare white summits of the Snowmass wilderness area.

Dropping down to the right, or north, from the top of *Sam's Knob* is the *Campground* area, an important part of the Snowmass skiing spectrum. These are long elegant runs, all marked black on the map, although they would be "dark" blue almost anywhere else. Runs like *Slot*, *Campground* and *Wildcat* are the finest sustained upper-intermediate

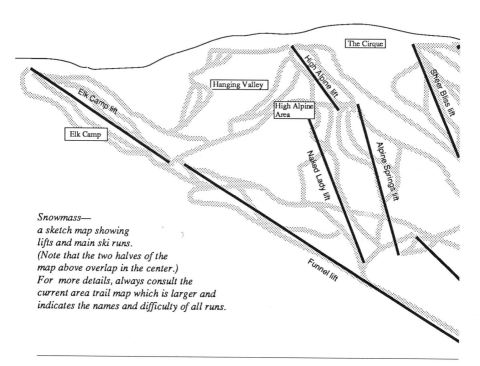

Snowmass—
a sketch map showing
lifts and main ski runs.
(Note that the two halves of the
map above overlap in the center.)
For more details, always consult the
current area trail map which is larger and
indicates the names and difficulty of all runs.

skiing on the whole mountain – pure fall lines, continuous pitches, runs
that go on and on and on.... This is perhaps the time to say that all
Snowmass runs are a little over-graded: a lot of Blues should be Greens,
a lot of Blacks should be Blues; and some of the double diamond Blacks
could be normal black slopes. But I think they've done this on purpose.
It's far better than the opposite, under-ranking of runs, which can get
skiers into real trouble. The Snowmass approach tends to make you feel
like a better skier than you really are. But isn't that what we all want?
And isn't that what all great mountains do, one way or another?

On the other, southeastern side of *Sam's Knob* is the next zone, the
Big Burn. It starts with the *Burn* itself and extends across eastward until
it reaches a great scooped out hollow in the middle of Snowmass mountain, the *Cirque*, a romantic windswept alpine basin that sits (almost
unskied) like a parenthesis in the center of an otherwise continuous
rigdeline, interrupting the smooth succession of runs across the upper
face.

The *Big Burn* itself has a number of named lines indicated like

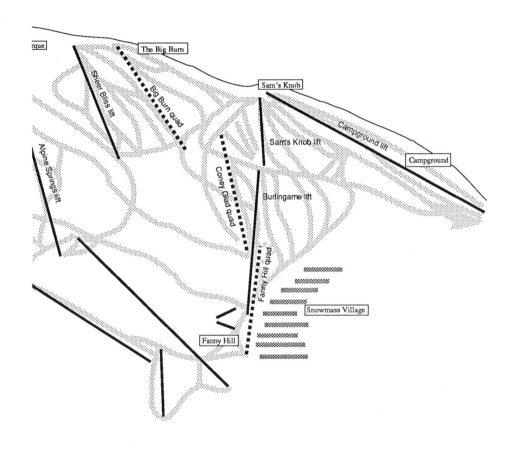

regular ski runs on the Trail Map, *Wineskin, Dallas Freeway, Timber-line*, etc... but to me these names seem artificial. The beauty of this terrain, which is not steep but simply vast, is that you can ski anywhere and everywhere, without once encountering the sort of obstacles, natural or man-made, that so often delimit the edges of a run or trail. Even more remarkable, really, is the terrain just east of the *Burn* itself, served by the Sheer Bliss lift. *Coyote Hollow* and *Sheer Bliss* are not the result of a long-ago forest fire but instead represent the finest job of man-made glading I think I've ever seen. Given enough money, manpower, and Forest Service permission, it's relatively easy to create wide-open treeless slopes. It's a lot harder to create slopes that still have a forested feel to them but which ski as if they were wide-open treeless slopes. That's exactly what you'll find on both sides of the Sheer Bliss lift! It's also a good deal harder to groom such gladed mountainsides; but they do it at Snowmass, after the first fresh blanket of powder has been tracked up; and typically they do it well.

Next door, to the east, the *Cirque* scoops out a big gap in the mountain (and the mountain's development). And beyond that we reach the *High Alpine* pod. At *High Alpine* you already feel as though you are a long long way from the village, and there's still one more skiing zone to go: *Elk Camp*, a low-angle novice paradise still further east. *High Alpine* has two personalities: a lower section served by the Alpine Springs and Naked Lady lifts with a lot of fairly ordinary ho-hum sort of blue runs: lots of mileage but not much charm and character; and an upper section, served by the High Alpine lift, which is terrific. This upper zone contains some moderately steep and very pleasant bump skiing, one long and roundabout "blue" adventure (ironically named *Green Cabin*) that winds its way into and down the side of the *Cirque*, and is the gateway to the most exciting terrain at Snowmass, the *Hanging Valley*. Although you ride the High Alpine lift to get there, *Hanging Valley* is a separate world that we'll look at in more detail a little later.

I've already mentioned *Elk Camp*, last stop on our west-to-east trip across the mountain. It's strictly a one shot deal, one lift, one type of skier: comfortable, easy practice runs that are marked blue but wouldn't have produced a single lifted eyebrow if they had been graded green. *Elk Camp* is connected back to the Village via a long diagonal boulevard of a run called the *Funnel*, and in the opposite sense by the very long Funnel chairlift – a fun route to coast home in the evening, but a lift to avoid at all costs: too long, too slow and too cold in mid winter.

Now that I've given you a hint of this mountain's size, and a way of breaking it up into sub-mountains, let's look at some special places and special strategies for different sorts of skiers.

SNOWMASS FOR LEARNING SKIERS

It's not fair to say that Snowmass has better learning terrain than Buttermilk, it just has a lot more of it. Newcomers will be initiated into the friendly mysteries of snow sliding on *Fanny Hill*, doubtless in a ski school context, which is always the best way to go. But once skiers have acquired even a modest repertoire of basic moves they can move around far easier on Snowmass mountain than at most other big

Colorado areas, where novices are often confined to small ghettos, and have trouble skiing the "whole mountain." This is actually a better mountain for novices than the trail map indicates.

In fact, a close look at the map doesn't reveal too many green runs. The two most obvious are the *Funnel* (via *Funnel Bypass*) and a meandering green route down from the top of *Sam's Knob* (*Max Park* to *Lunchline* to *Dawdler*). But at Snowmass many of the blue runs are so friendly and well groomed that skiers who normally have to look for the easiest way down can handle them with ease. But which blue runs? In a way the trail marking system breaks down here, because some blue runs are so easy, while others are more demanding and serious. Since the map doesn't make these fine distinctions, I will.

I've already mentioned that the entire *Elk Camp* area is very, very gentle. Anyone who can make some sort of skidded turn will be comfortable here. To reach either *Elk Camp* or the *Funnel*, novices can ride lifts 11 and 15 (the Wood Run and Naked Lady chairs) then traverse across on *Turkey Trot*, a very easy Blue. Also on the eastern side of the mountain, *Adams Avenue* and *Green Cabin* (from High Alpine down!) are barely in the blue category and should present no problems to unskilled skiers. Back on the main flank of the mountain above the village, novice skiers can also escape from their green-only world by making a big loop from the top of *Sam's Knob* via *Trestle* (a short, friendly road) and the lower portion of *Green Cabin*. But novices should avoid the blue runs on the front face of *Sam's Knob*, which are all rather serious. How about the *Big Burn* for inexperienced skiers? Not really recommended, but you can do it for thrills, if you remember that there's no rule that says you have to ski straight down a slope. The *Burn* is wide enough to allow inexperienced skiers to negotiate it via very long side-to-side traverses and relatively few turns. It's wide enough too that such "behavior" won't get in the way of other, better skiers.

SNOWMASS FOR "CRUISERS"

Like Vail, Snowmass is a cruising mountain par excellence. In skiers' lingo, "cruising" has a special, even privileged sense. A cruising skier is at one with the terrain, not struggling, not solving problems, not even responding to challenges but simply savoring the rush of snow, air, speed. A cruiser prefers the natural lines that the mountain offers, takes them and flows. Cruising is not showing off, not carving your initials on the snow in a series of short, precise, snappy arcs, not going for big air in the bumps under the lift. The cruiser instinctively dials in big turns, long smoothly blended curves, heads for open spaces and prefers a steady non-stop pace down the mountain. Does it sound like fun? It would be easy to argue that cruising is the most fun you can have on skis; and Snowmass is a good place for you to find out if it's true.

Where will the cruiser find true happiness on this mountain? The Big Burn and Sheer Bliss lifts are cruising headquarters. It's easy to spot the most popular lines here, and easy to consciously ski away from them so that a touch of extra speed won't disturb other skiers – elementary cruising courtesy. There's no reason a creative skier couldn't cruise these two lifts all day without ever repeating exactly the same line. Next to the *Burn* I'll nominate *Slot* and *Wildcat* over on the *Campground* side as cruisers' heaven. A lot of skiers are hesitant to let their skis run on the somewhat steeper pitches of the *Campground* runs. But by drawing out the end of each turn into an arc across, rather than down the hill, one can turn even a steeply tilted slope into a cruiser's delight. Provided there's enough room; and room is no problem on any of the *Campground* runs. (For more cruising tips, see the next *Ski Tech* section.) Unfortunately, *Sam's Knob* introduces a short uphill stretch into the otherwise continuous slope between the *Big Burn* and *Campground*. But by schussing the last slopes of Sneaky's, keeping your speed up, and cutting south saround the Knob itself, you can put together a truly enormous and memorable cruising run, continuing on down to the bottom of the Campground lift in one fell thigh-burning swoop.

The blue runs of the *Alpine Springs* area are less interesting, less open and less exciting for serious cruising than the western side of the mountain (they're also less crowded). But since these runs are cut through dense forest, you'll find both better visibility and more sheltered conditions over here on stormy days. There's nothing wrong with the "front" terrain on *Sam's Knob* for cruising except that this is typically a high traffic area, and fast skiing and crowds don't mix.

SNOWMASS FOR ADVENTURE

Don't get the idea that Snowmass is a cruising mountain because it lacks steeper, harder slopes. You can find pitches here that will wake you up, make you concentrate and leave you feeling proud of yourself after a successful run. There isn't a lot of hard skiing at Snowmass, which is fine on such a balanced mountain because only a minority of skiers are looking for that kind of excitement. But there's enough to keep that minority happy.

The biggest thrills at Snowmass are found in the high alpine terrain of the *Cirque* and *Hanging Valley*. From the top of the Sheer Bliss lift (chair 9), you can ski down along the edge of the *Cirque*, the large central amphitheater that looks like it was scooped out of the Snowmass ridge with a giant ice-cream scooper. The left (western) bank of this hole in the mountain is formed by a long series of cliffs, but there are a couple of ways through, gaps in the wall, and they're bloody exciting. Signs and ropes will lead you to *KT Gully* and *Rock Island*, which deserve their double black diamond designations. Once you have performed your obligatory short-swing dance down these steep gullies, the skiing mellows out as you slide down to *Green Cabin*. Even more stimulating is *AMF* a steep alpine gully dropping into the very top of the *Cirque*. *AMF* is a local tag not found on the trail map, that may stand for *Adios My Friend....* The best route back up to *AMF* is to ski all the way down to the Cony Glade quad and take it and the Burn quad back up. (These new lifts are so rapid, that it's often better to ski further down the mountain in order to ride faster lifts back up). Next door to *AMF* is an even steeper gully, *Goudy's*, sometimes called *80/20* because 80% of the skiers who look over the edge chicken out.

Even finer, longer, and more remote are the runs from the top of the High Alpine chair into *Hanging Valley*. These runs are also marked with double black diamonds; and while all the terrain back here isn't terribly difficult, this area is so remote and dramatic that such a rating is certainly fair. It was an enlightened move to open *Hanging Valley* to the skiing public; for many years the Snowmass ski patrol had kept it to themselves as a kind of insiders' powder preserve. It's a difficult and remote area to control, patrol and sweep, a sort of "in-bounds" out-back situation. *Hanging Valley* gives Snowmass a dimension it would otherwise totally lack. You can see them up there – these beautiful steep alpine slopes – overhanging the gentle cruising trails of *Elk Camp* like a perpetual dare, telling Snowmass skiers: no matter how good you become, there'll always be a challenge waiting for you. Nice.

The *Hanging Valley Wall* is a longer, more intriguing route than the *Hanging Valley Glades* that branch to the right off a normal black bump slope, *The Edge*, on the High Alpine lift. The extra ten minutes you'll spend walking east from the top of the High Alpine chair to the *Wall* is well worth it. The Wall is a two-step affair, the first pitch is a steep but short face that drops you from a high bare ridge down onto a timbered bench in the middle of nowhere. There seem to be a lot of choices here, and at first, one has the impression that there is more vertical and more powder to be had by trending right down the second, longer step. In fact, you're better off to head left dropping down along the left edge of the final high wall until you spot your perfect line. The pitches on this lower face are known as *Wall 1*, *Wall 2*, *Strawberry Patch*, *Cassidy's* and *Union 1 & 2*. (It's nice to talk the same language as the locals.) *Hanging Valley* is real adventure terrain: there are no trail signs, warning signs or other "ski area" type information back here. If you're hesitating, the ski school also offers guided tours back here. Check at the ski school desk at the High Alpine restaurant.

Even here in the wilds of *Hanging Valley*, the ski area has been hard at work. The reason it's so easy to reach the best lines on the *Wall* is because the forest along its edge has been discreetly thinned. Even when you fly out across the rolling flats where the *Wall* joins *Sandy Park*, you will owe your last dozen turns to the efficient, almost invisible glading that the ski area has done in summer. Good work guys!

There are numerous control ropes in this area, and also beneath the big *Cirque*. At first they don't seem to make sense, since you can sometimes spot runs coming in on both sides of the ropes. These are not really closure ropes but rather control ropes that separate different areas, which the patrol has to check and sweep at different times – so it's important to respect them. They're not just put there to bug you.

While strong intermediate and advanced skiers will tend to head for the *Big Burn* on a powder morning, expert skiers should strike out for the *Wall*, ASAP. The quickest way to get there from the village is to take theWood Run, Alpine Springs and High Alpine chairs in succession. If you head for the *Wall* via the super quads up the front, it may be tracked up by the time you get there. Check the double-black-diamond status boards at the bottoms of the Sheer Bliss and High Alpine chairs to see what's open.

SNOWMASS AND THE FUTURE

As good a mountain as Snowmass is, it's still not perfect, that is to say, it's not yet finished. Improvements like the recent super chairs are just part of an ambitious program of mountain expansion and improvement that involves new lifts and runs on the eastern, *Elk Camp* and *Hanging Valley* end of the mountain. The *Cirque* and the treeless slopes above it could be opened up with surface lifts. Even more exciting, and the only reason I'm ending my Snowmass chapter in the future tense is the possibility of linking Snowmass to Buttermilk via Burnt Mountain, a kind of miniature Snowmass lying between the two. With new super quad lifts, this link-up is no longer a pipe dream. It would create an awesome mega-area with one base in the Roaring Fork Valley just outside Aspen, and add the possibility of European-style village-to-village skiing to the Aspen ski scene. Will the Skiing Company do it? Let's keep our fingers crossed.

SNOWMASS DATA

KEY PHONE NUMBERS

Central Reservations   800-525-6200

TRANSPORTATION

By car, 4 hour drive from Denver on I-70 to Glenwood Springs, then
        south on Highway 82 (in good road and weather
        conditions).
By bus or limo, or High Mountain Taxi (vans) from Denver's Stapleton
        Airport.
By plane, via Continental Express or United Express from Denver's
        Stapleton Airport to Aspen. Also non-stop jet flights
        from several major cities.
Free shuttle bus from downtown Aspen

MOUNTAIN STATISTICS

Vertical Drop	3,615 feet
Summit Elev.	11,835 feet
Base Elevation	8,220 feet
Skiing Terrain	2,099 acres
Longest Run	3.7 miles
Number of Lifts	16 including, 3 high-speed detachable quad chairs
Uphill Capacity	20,535 skiers per hour
Snowboarding	Yes

Snowmass lift tickets are good at Aspen & Buttermilk. A ticket good at
        all 4 Aspen areas can also be purchased.

The cruiser's secret weapon is an effortless, energy-saving, long-radius turn – more elegant and more efficient than the way most intermediate skiers hack their way down the slope. To ski this way, you'll need two skills: a smoother beginning to your turn, and means of controlling your speed that doesn't depend on skidding or digging your edges into the snow.

A smoother start to the turn. *Having polished up the arc or trajectory of your turn by learning to ride that outside ski exclusively, your next step is to start into the turn with less oomph, less effort. If you just twist, swing, or throw your skis around sideways, you're not only wearing yourself out, you make it harder for the ski to follow its own bent curve in the snow. You'll skid down the mountain in short bursts of motion rather than cruising it in big effortless arcs. The ideal cruising turn starts slowly, progressively, with the skis peeling gradually off into an arc, not jammed quickly around the corner. How does it work?*

The pure smooth start to your parallel turn depends on early weight shift. Most skiers try to turn their skis and feet before they shift weight to the outside ski. I'm going to ask you to try a very curious thing: stand on your new outside foot before you twist it into the turn. At first, you won't be able to do this on a steep or impressive slope. Play with this idea on wide-open, gentle green runs just to see what it's like. Shift your weight first, then turn. Surprise – the start of the turn will take more time. And because you're already standing on the top, soon-to-be-outside ski of the turn, you won't be able to twist it as much. The turn itself will slow down, and you'll find yourself carving a cleaner, longer arc. As the habit develops you will notice that even when you get in trouble, even on steep slopes, even in bumps, as long as you shift your weight onto the new ski before turning, then both skis will always pivot smoothly together into the new turn. (That's right, it really is the top ski I want you to step on before turning downhill.)

Completing the arc of the turn by remaining on that outside ski. The sophisticated skier's method for controlling speed.

Speed control. *Speed control in a long radius turn is easy – if you simply keep on turning. And that's easy. As long as you keep all your weight on your outside ski, the bent shape of the ski will keep it turning. As soon as you equalize your weight on both skis, the turning action disappears. But how about speed control? Long-radius turns give you more time in the fall line to pick up speed, so slowing down at the end of each turn is important. The theory is simple: if your ski keeps turning, it will eventually turn up hill and bring you to a stop. Even if you don't turn that far, the slope is still decreasing underfoot, so it is the shape of the hill, and not the resistance from your edges digging into the snow that slows you down. Speed control by "completing the turn." Turning longer, rather than harder. This is, in fact, the way that expert skiers control their speed – by guiding their skis further around the arc, rather than by scraping, skidding and edging. And you can too. Smooth, long, round turns – pure pleasure.*

PART III   NORTH FROM DENVER

CHAPTER 6   STEAMBOAT

Steamboat, which I rank right after Vail and Aspen in quality and importance as a Colorado ski resort, is a bit of an enigma – to me and to a lot of skiers. The real mystery, I guess, is why Steamboat has worked so hard to craft an old-time Western image for itself, an image composed of cowboy hats and chaps, horses belly deep in snow, and soulful old barns, a kind of daguerreotype frozen on the pages of ski magazines and in skiers' minds – but an image that doesn't have much to do with Steamboat skiing. Steamboat skiing is thoroughly modern, simply outrageous.

Steamboat is a giant of a ski mountain. I just never suspected how big it was and how much skiing it offered, until I finally visited Steamboat many years after I moved to Colorado. (My only excuse for waiting so long is that I settled in the southwest corner of the state, while Steamboat, by contrast, is the most northwestern of Colorado resorts. A poor excuse.) It was a wonderful surprise. Steamboat is a far better ski resort than any of its ad campaigns, or indeed anything I've ever seen written about it, would lead you to believe.

The western metaphor, I suppose, is a natural one because the town of Steamboat Springs – not right next to the ski area, but a few miles away – really is a regional ranching center, a market town for cattle raisers up and down the wide Yampa valley. But Wild West it ain't. It is a traditional western strip town with a long main street; yet there are few historical touches, no cutsey false fronts and, thank god, no staged shoot-outs for tourists on the main drag. The town of Steamboat Springs is an everyday working western town not a show western town, which means that downtown you're going to see more Cummings Diesel and John Deere "gimmie hats" than Stetsons. This town is a big part of the story of Steamboat skiing, but no longer a big part of skiers' vacation experience here.

As Steamboat has matured as a ski resort, a brand new ski village has grown up at the base of Mt. Werner and its lifts. A village that is far more ski-contemporary than historic-western. You no longer, as in Steamboat's early years, have to go "downtown" for a good meal or a little apres-ski action, it's just one more option. But the most interesting options at Steamboat are up on the ski mountain. This is not a mountain that provides merely good skiing but – you can quote me – great skiing. And that's where we'll start our guided tour.

THE LOOK AND FEEL OF THE MOUNTAIN

Steamboat's ski mountain is often loosely referred to as Mt. Werner, even though the real summit of Mt. Werner sits above and behind the current area. You can see most of the mountain from the flat rolling ranch country of the Yampa valley below – a series of massive steps covered with a frosted net of white ribbon runs. But it's almost impossible to guess the scale, to know how much you're seeing at once, or how far away those top runs really are.

I think of Steamboat's mountain in three parts: the lower mountain and the two separate sides or halves of the upper mountain. The lower mountain is a kind of frontal peak called Thunderhead. There are a number of chairlifts scattered over the slopes of this lower peak, but the main route up to Thunderhead is via Steamboat's 8-person Swiss gondola, the Silver Bullet (the ride is rapid, only 9 minutes, and the vertical significant, 2,200 feet). You walk out of the Thunderhead gondola terminal, and realize you are still separated from the upper slopes by a kind of long rounded saddle. Instead of going right on up, you must ski down a ways into one of the basins on either side of this high Thunderhead saddle.

Decisions, decisions: right or left? If you ski down to the left, you'll reach chairlifts that take you up on the slopes of Storm Peak, the lefthand or northernmost of Steamboat's twin upper summits. If you ski down to the right side, you'll reach lifts that take you up the righthand or southern summit of the upper mountain, Sunshine Peak. So far so good: one large lower mountain, sitting out in front of two broad upper peaks. Each of these different "mountains" functions as a separate ski domain with its own character, its own views, its own type of skiing. And each of these "mountains on the mountain" feels about as big as many respectable-sized ski areas.

It's possible to ski across from the Storm Peak side to the Sunshine Peak side, and vice versa, once you're up there. But the natural tendency is to ski on one side or the other, and then take a comeback chairlift back up to Thunderhead Saddle. Then it's decision time again: visit the opposite side of the upper mountain, ski on the lower slopes, or lunch in one of the various restaurants in the massive Thunderhead gondola building.

The mountain below Thunderhead has an enormous amount of good skiing on it, and if there weren't something about human nature that makes us all want to head for the summits, this lower mountain could hold your attention all day. At first you'll probably just ski down it in the evening. But it's worth some serious exploration during your week at Steamboat. And of course, we'll go on to explore all three zones of the mountain in more detail in the next sections, focused on different levels of skiers.

But I mentioned "your week" at Steamboat, because this is definitely a vacation not a weekend ski resort. Even though the drive from Denver and Colorado's front range cities isn't that much longer than the drive to Summit county resorts (like Breckenridge, Copper and Keystone), it is widely perceived as both much longer and tougher. So weekend skiers just don't seem to come here, at least not in any significant numbers. And this yields a number of very pleasant bonuses at Steamboat. First, there are no big ugly parking lots scattered around the base of the mountain to absorb waves of weekend visitors, and undermine both the resort's architecture and the mountain views. (There are a couple of discreet and quite adequate parking structures, and of course, most lodging units have their own self contained parking.) And second, with steadier, more evenly distributed skier numbers to serve, Steamboat has done a very unusual job of upgrading its lift facilities. Like other major Colorado resorts, Steamboat too has tried to eliminate lift lines – and pretty much succeeded. But they've managed to do it without installing a single detachable quad chair. This is interesting because the conventional wisdom has it that high-speed detachables are the only way to beat lift lines.

At Steamboat, they've updated their lift system with a lot of fast (but not super-fast) modern triple chairs, often installed in tandem with earlier lifts or placed in unlikely but strategic spots, so as to give skiers more options and eliminate those natural bottlenecks where everybody skis down into a *cul de sac* from which there's only one direction, and one chairlift, out. Bravo Steamboat! Thanks for demonstrating that intelligent mountain design can do just as much as multi-million dollar detachables in improving skier access. The intelligence of the lift layout makes the beautifully designed electronic lift status boards almost redundant; but they're a splendid example of modern ski area signage.

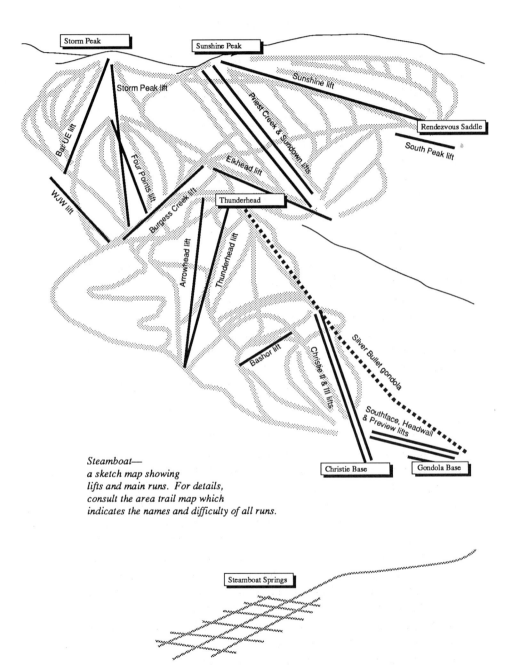

Steamboat—
a sketch map showing
lifts and main runs. For details,
consult the area trail map which
indicates the names and difficulty of all runs.

And finally before leaving the subject of lifts, I'll add that somebody should be praised for painting Steamboat's lift towers a deep, rich midnight blue that seems to come right out of the dark north Colorado sky.

Dramatic color and its corollary, dramatic light, are part of the everyday Steamboat ski experience because of a natural fluke. This mountain faces west! Most ski areas are laid out facing primarily north which guarantees cold dry snow conditions but also keeps many slopes gray and somber. On a primarily west-facing peak like Steamboat, the afternoon light is more intense and golden, and even the morning shadows seem deeper and more dramatic. Yet Steamboat is high enough, and far enough north, that its snow conditions don't seem to suffer from this western orientation. And the view from the mountain – a wide westerly panorama of broad white valleys and rolling, receding, snow-crusted foothills, a view that stretches on and on because there are no high peaks to the West – is actually enhanced, because there are no bare south-facing slopes anywhere to be seen. This stunning view, by the way, seems to be built-in to just about every run on the mountain.

Which brings me to a final observation before we look in detail at particular runs for particular skiers. Every ski mountain has its own feel, its own flavor, its own atmosphere – the result of a hard-to-analyze combination of snow conditions, terrain, scenery, trail design, even the attitudes of skier service personnel like lift operators. Two mountains with the same statistics, vertical drop, uphill capacity etc, can have a completely different feel. What I want to say is that Steamboat has a wonderful feel. When I try to pin it down, remembering great days at Steamboat, I come up with two or three special qualities: The steady continuous nature of most runs. They go on and on in long uninterrupted pitches, not in fits and starts, not in flats and drops, not in sudden constrictions and sudden widenings, but in a long, smooth, satisfying flow. Then there are the wide, plunging views that I've already mentioned – that suspended-in-the-sky feeling that makes skiers feel like privileged characters (which they certainly are). And finally there are the aspen trees. Steamboat is not as high as other resorts further south, and so its magnificent aspen stands grow right to the top of Sunshine Peak (10,385 ft.). These aspen groves, we'll see, are incredible to ski through, but they're also fabulous to look at. Taller, whiter, straighter than aspens on other Colorado ski mountains, with lacy, fringy tops that seem to glow against the deep winter sky. Aspens are everywhere on this mountain; like no trees you've ever seen.

But now for some specifics:

STEAMBOAT FOR WEAKER SKIERS

Steamboat is not a mountain with a lot of "green" showing on its
trail map; in fact, there are almost no green runs at all on what I've
called the upper mountain. Not to worry. There is a wonderful area on
top of the mountain, that's only nominally blue, which is very accessible
to less experienced skiers. I mean the runs on the far side of the Sunshine lift, especially *Tomahawk* and *Quickdraw* and the short connecting
runs between them, so low-key and friendly that locals call this zone
"Wally World." I wouldn't hesitate to recommend these slopes to
inexperienced skiers who normally stick to green runs, but who still
want to experience the whole mountain. These runs are long, gentle,
extremely wide, and I don't see how anyone who can make some kind of
sloppy skidded christy can get into trouble up there – provided you take
the right route down the mountain. To exit Wally World in one piece,
novices should be sure to take *Duster*, a cross-mountain catwalk, from
near the Rendezvous Saddle house (Ragnar's Restaurant). It cuts across
the mountain behind Thunderhead peak, eventually turning into a
greenish run called *Park Lane* that connects with several easy ways
down the lower mountain (all green slopes).

There are a lot more green practice runs on the lower mountain,
especially from the top of the Christie chairs. Two long green trails,
B C Ski Way and the more interesting, *Why Not*, that wind their way
completely around the lower mountain, can be reached from the top of
the Silver Bullet gondola. There's also a super beginner area at the base
of the mountain served by a double and a triple chair plus a mighty-
might drag lift, which is where the ski school starts their never-evers

STEAMBOAT FOR GOOD SKIERS

Somewhere past parallel, when cruising fever takes hold, Steamboat
skiing really starts to get exciting. *Buddy's Run* from the top of Storm
Peak is a favorite: lots of room, lots of variations. No pressure to turn
here, there, or any particular spot. No reason not to accept a bit more
speed. This classic cruiser, along with runs like *High Noon* on the
Sunshine Peak side, and *Heavenly Daze* on the front face of the lower
mountain, spells bliss for strong skiers who just don't want to bother
with short turns, with putting on the brakes , above all with bumps. But
there are also a lot of black runs at Steamboat that are just plain inviting,
that really don't require expert skiing skills at all. I'm thinking of black
runs like *The Ridge* and *Cowtrack* on Storm Peak, and *Valley View*
below Thunderhead, that do require short turns and fall-line skiing, but
never seem to throw awkwardly shaped bumps in your way. And if it's

friendly bumps you're searching for, you'll often find them on *Twilight*, *One O'clock* and *Two O'clock*, slightly steeper lines that drop down and right from *High Noon*, over on the Sunshine Peak side.

STEAMBOAT FOR EXPERTS

A great ski mountain should get better and better as skiers get better and better. Steamboat qualifies. If you're an expert or near-expert skier, you'll go nuts here. I don't necessarily mean a hero, a hot shot with rubber knees and thunder thighs, but simply a very strong skier, a skier who's at home on moderately steep bumps, comfortable in powder, capable of turning not just where you want to, but where you need to. A lot of skiers fit this description. It's a reasonable, practical goal that I really believe most skiers can achieve with enough patience, enough practice. (In fact, my earlier book *Breakthrough on Skis* was is based on this assumption, and sets out a pretty straightforward path to expert skiing.) Just what does Steamboat reserve for expert skiers? Powder and trees, often both together. And the combination is dynamite.

There are a fair number of exciting black runs, steep and moguled, on both the upper and lower mountain. But Steamboat's most exciting skiing is found among the aspen trees. For some reason, the slender white aspen trunks on this mountain are almost perfectly spaced. Enough room between them for good skiers to weave through these forests without feeling pinched, pressured, wondering if you're "going to make it." These classic, open aspen lines abound in the *Priest Creek* area, on the Sunshine Peak side of the upper mountain. *Priest Creek* used to be a kind of locals' preserve, but then a second lift was put in here and several open lines to the right of the new lift, as well as the lift lines themselves, were actually widened into proper, treeless runs. Paradise lost, wailed a few die-hards, but it's not true. There is still an enormous amount of lovely, exciting, tree skiing up here, right in the heart of the open aspen forest. The angle steepens a bit and skiing is a more exciting to the north of Sundown and Priest Creek lifts, where the two main lines you'll see on the trail map, *Shadows* and *Closet*, are only generalized areas, not clearly defined runs.

Good short turns are a must. In periods between storms, you'll even encounter moguls, not mean moguls but still moguls, amongst these trees. But I repeat Steamboat tree skiing is not just for heroes, these are actually the easiest forests to ski in the state. For a strong skier, the experience involves far more pleasure than challenge.

I talked about trees and powder. Steamboat tends to catch northern storms out of Wyoming that sometimes miss central and southern

Colorado resorts. Next to Vail's Back Bowls, a lot of skiers think that Steamboat offers the best powder skiing in the state. And the combination of trees and powder creates an experience that's greater than the sum of its parts. Steamboat's western orientation, and the typical westerly winds that accompany big storms, transform the aspen forests into fairy groves, white trees festooned with white hoarfrost, white lace – incredible!

For unusual tree skiing, and perhaps some stashes of late powder long after *Priest Creek* is tracked out, explore the forest zones in between the zig-zags of *Why Not*, an easy green comeback trail on the lower mountain – some of the best tree skiing at Steamboat.

MOUNTAIN MISCELLANY

Most days, it makes more sense to eat lunch up on the mountain than to ski back down to the base village for lunch. There are two mountain restaurant locations but considerably more than two restaurants to chose from. At Rendezvous Saddle below the Sunshine chair you'll find a regular mountain cafeteria, barbecue on the deck, and the mountain's most popular sit-down restaurant, Ragnar's. It's worth eating at Ragnar's just for the wild Norwegian names on the menu. Try the *Fyldt Pandekager* (shrimp crepes) or the *Stekt Rødspaette Trondheim* (sauteed sole with asparagus and leeks). At Thunderhead, the massive mid-mountain crossroads at the top of the Silver Bullet gondola, there were at least four separate restaurant/cafeteria facilities last time I counted, where the fare includes Mexican, Italian, mid-American, country & western, a Pizza bar, a barbecue deck, etc. The fancier of the two sit-down restaurants at Thunderhead, Hazie's, competes head-to-head with Ragnar's with a menu full of gourmet overtones. But you can also ride the gondola up here in the evening and combine a meal at Hazie's with a knockout view of the Yampa valley and Steamboat Springs sparkling below – which makes more sense to me than lunch.

THE VILLAGE, A FEW HOT TIPS

Shall I be honest? Why not. Steamboat is definitely a mountain to fall in love with, but there is nothing about the village – either the newish ski village at the base of Mt. Werner or old town Steamboat, a few miles away – to make you lose your head. In fact, the base village is pretty nice: good facilities, good hotels, lodges and condo-style units, a good selection of eateries, sport stores, conventional and even off-beat shops, good service by locals with a good attitude, in short all the amenities you'd expect at a first class Rocky Mountain ski resort, which

Steamboat definitely is. But not a lot of character, character that could make Steamboat, the place, feel as different from other Colorado resorts as Steamboat, the mountain, feels different from other Colorado ski mountains.

Don't be discouraged, every great ski mountain can't have a great village at its base (and vice versa), a good one is quite sufficient.

I like the ski village (officially Steamboat Village) because it functions as a pedestrian environment. Cars are out of sight and unneeded. The main centers at the base of the ski mountain, Gondola Square and Ski Time Square, are integrated multi-level plazas and arcades. You can easily stroll from one cluster of activity to another in minutes. And it will probably be several nights before you've explored the ski village thoroughly enough to be tempted by the ten minute drive into "downtown" Steamboat Springs.

A few favorites: "The Butcher Shop," a hard to find steak house in Ski Time Square that's worth the trouble of finding. Club Majiks, a dinner/cabaret club in the Clock Tower at Ski Time Square. And in downtown Steamboat, l'Apogée for dinner.

Lodging at the base of the mountain is mainly in stylish modern condo/apartment blocks, all within easy walking distance of the slopes. There is even a newish Sheraton Hotel, a full-service extravaganza, that looks as if it had been transplanted intact from a Florida golf resort. Of course, one advantage of having an honestly working-class western ranch town nearby is that one can organize a week's lodging at almost any price range imaginable, from slopeside deluxe to a modest motel. And I suppose that's the flip side, the plus side, of my comment about Steamboat's town and village not having as much unique character as its mountain. No one could call Steamboat pretentious, or precious. Nor is it self-consciously pricey. The town of Steamboat may be hard to fall in love with, but it's easy to enjoy.

STEAMBOAT DATA

KEY PHONE NUMBERS

Snow Conditions		(303) 879-7300
Ski Area Information		1-800-332-3204
	also:	(303) 879-6111 (in state)
Central Reservations		1-800-922-2722
	also:	(303) 332-3204 (in state)

TRANSPORTATION

By car, 3 hour drive (in good road and weather conditions) from Denver on I-70 to Silverthorn exit, then north on Colorado Highway 9 to Kremmling, then west on US 40 to Steamboat.

By shuttle or limo or taxi, from the Bob Adams STOL-port and the Yampa Valley Regional Airport. Rental cars also available at both airports.

By plane, via Continental Express from Denver to the Bob Adams STOL-port (3 miles from the resort); daily non-stop scheduled service from many cities to Yampa Valley Regional Airport (22 miles from the resort).

MOUNTAIN STATISTICS

Vertical Drop	3,600 feet
Summit Elev.	10,500 feet
Base Elevation	6,900 feet
Skiing Terrain	2,500 acres
Longest Run	3 miles
Number of Lifts	20 including, one gondola and 1 surface lift
Uphill Capacity	28,730 skiers per hour
Snowboarding	yes

SKI TECH: *TREES WITHOUT FEAR*

For most of this last chapter I've been raving about the beauty of Steamboat's trees, aspen glades universally considered the finest tree-skiing in the state. But I know that not everyone feels at home among these tall, white trunks. By comparison with the middle of a large well groomed run, tree skiing – even friendly Steamboat style tree skiing – can seem cramped, restrictive, and with so many arboreal obstacles, downright intimidating. Here are a few tips to help you make peace with these noble trees.

True, you need good short turns to ski among trees. An anticipated style, upper body pretty quiet, aimed more-or-less down the hill, while legs and skis turn from side to side beneath you, and above all, a rapid decisive pole plant. The pole plant is the trigger that launches a good short turn, and if you hesitate with your pole, you'll probably hesitate to turn too, and woops! here comes that big tree trunk.

To ski well among trees, tight trees or wide-spaced Steamboat trees you have to plan ahead, and you have to get rid of that "what if" anxiety. What if I don't make the next turn, what if I hit a tree. You won't. Because if you're about to hit a tree you can just sit down in the snow. Not very elegant to be sure, but very secure. You won't be skiing at high speeds among trees, so you can always "save yourself" from disaster by just bailing out and sitting down. Once you realize this, and maybe do it once or twice, you really won't worry about hitting trees anymore. And as I've said, Steamboat has some of the friendliest, most widely spaced aspen groves in the west. Almost too easy.

Like a chess player, you'll want to plot your strategy several moves – or turns – in advance. Look up. Look ahead, And keep adjusting your line to take you toward the widest gaps between tree trunks. If you look at your ski tips, you're lost.

Any time you're skiing through or near trees, you should also make a point of taking the straps of your ski poles off your wrists. If you snag a pole on a twig or branch, this will keep you from spraining your wrist, or worse.

And finally at an area where tree skiing is as popular as it is at Steamboat, you'll often find moguls between the trees. What then? No big deal, simply use these moguls – incipient or fully formed – to ski with less effort than you might otherwise. By always initiating your turns on the high spot or crest of the bump, which serves as a pivot point, you can turn with far less speed than you usually use. And while you're getting used to navigating through trees, less speed is a blessing. It gives you that much more time to look ahead and plan your route through these giant, inflexible slalom poles.

In Colorado skiing, Winter Park is an exception to the norm in more ways than one. It's a very big ski mountain (three mountains really) in terms of size and number of visitors, but somehow it's never become a truly romantic ski-vacation destination. Winter Park is a publicly owned ski area (owned by the city of Denver) with a wonderful management philosophy, focused exclusively on delivering the best ski experience for the best price rather than playing a real-estate game in parallel with ski-area operations, as is so often the case. Winter Park is a mecca for expert skiers in search of a challenge, but also quite possibly introduces more beginners to the sport than any other Rocky mountain area. It has also developed the finest handicaped skier program in the country. Winter Park has ambitious expansion plans underway that may someday make it the biggest ski area in America, but in the meantime it's a helluva bargain. And it's probably the last area in the West you can ride a ski train to!

Winter Park lies just on the north side of Berthoud Pass. Well and good you ask, unless you're a native of Colorado, but where is Berthoud Pass? Berthoud Pass is a 11,315-ft. gap in the ranks of high, rounded, mountains lining both sides of Interstate 70, Colorado's main auto route across the Rockies. You branch off this freeway about halfway between Denver and the continental divide, turn north and zigzag up and over Berthoud pass through steep, densely timbered slopes. This is classic Colorado "Front Range" country: dark green mountains, narrow shadowy valleys, and for the motorist, slow and twisting roads. You wind down the far side of the pass, and just before exiting the mountains themselves onto the open rolling parklands that lead on north toward Steamboat, you stumble on Winter Park.

A novel approach, driving down to a ski area, and then, alerted only by a few big signs and a couple of visible ski runs through the trees, turning off a small highway onto a smaller "way" in search of the area's base facilities and parking lots. Nothing about one's arrival at Winter Park makes you think that it's really a big ski area. Let's look closer:

THE SHAPE AND FEEL OF THE MOUNTAIN

Most of Winter Park is out of sight from the bottom. From *either* bottom. Because, actually, there are two bases, and two distinct although interconnected zones. The main base area serves the original ski mountain, Winter Park proper. While the other base, back up the canyon a mile or so, and reached by a small road that winds quite a distance in from the highway, is known as Mary Jane, like the mountain it serves. In all fairness, I have to say that one can also think of Winter Park as being composed of three mountains, not two—since the Vasquez Ridge area at Winter Park seems to qualify as a separate peak. But for me the division into two "areas" makes more sense.

Mary Jane is not just the newer half of Winter Park, it is also the challenging half, where the easiest runs are serious blues, where the big bumps live. Mary Jane is almost entirely responsible for Winter Park's reputation among serious, hot young skiers. It is a two-sided mountain, whose summit can be accessed by any of three long chairs that run in parallel up its front face. The middle one, Summit Express, is a new high-speed detachable quad that gets most of the traffic, unless weekend skiers start filling its maze, and forcing skiers onto the Challenger and Iron Horse lifts, which are slower, traditional double chairs. Both sides of Mary Jane are equally steep, equally fierce or equally "interesting," depending on your point of view. What the trail map labels as Mary Jane's Backside is more the left flank of the mountain (looking up) than the back. In the past, all the runs on this "backside" funneled you onto a long, dull comeback road called Corona Way. But with the addition of a new chair, the Sunnyside lift, for the 89/90 season, it has become even more pleasant to ski back there.

Getting from one mountain to the other, or crossing back and forth between the two, demands a bit of forethought. The top of Mary Jane is higher than the Winter Park side, and the Mary Jane base is also higher than the Winter Park base. Thus you can easily ski down from the Mary Jane base to Winter Park's base, via a green trail, *The Corridor*, but not vice versa. This means that if you start your ski day on the Winter Park side, you'll enjoy greater freedom of movement around the mountain, with no problems returning to your car in late afternoon.

Winter Park itself is spread out and diffuse. It's a complexly laid out, ridgey sort of ski mountain that takes a while to get oriented to.

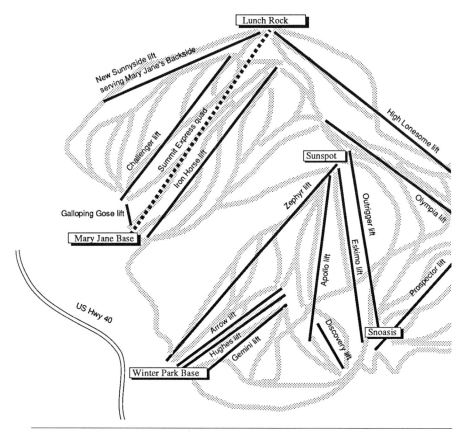

Every high point seems to offer alternative ski routes down alternate sides, so that after a while you lose the notion of front and back, realizing that this is a ski area that meanders over a number of separate ridges, down and along a number of separate valleys or drainages. The task of orientation isn't facilitated by the enthusiasm with which the mountain crew have baptized every single slot, opening, gap in the trees, or shortcut from one run to another with its own separate name. Thus the trail map lists 106 designated trails. Don't take this too seriously, Winter Park is big, but not that big! Still, it's worth trying to absorb an accurate overview of the mountain, because if you make the wrong choices you can waste a lot of time on endless flatish runs that seem to go nowhere, slowly.

A simplified overview of Winter Park (*sans* Mary Jane) would divide up into four zones: Directly above the base (I suppose that makes it the "front" face) is an area of steeper black and blue-black runs that are fairly serious. Although one notices, looking up from the base, that a

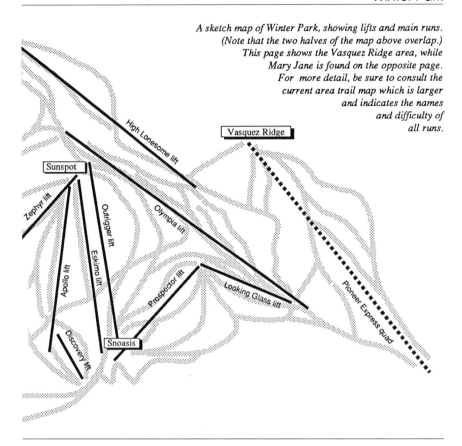

A sketch map of Winter Park, showing lifts and main runs. (Note that the two halves of the map above overlap.) This page shows the Vasquez Ridge area, while Mary Jane is found on the opposite page. For more detail, be sure to consult the current area trail map which is larger and indicates the names and difficulty of all runs.

number of easier runs are coming back in from the right side – from somewhere around the corner. Zephyr Lift takes you to the summit of this front zone and opens up the backside of the mountain, an altogether different sort of ski domain with lots of long, inviting, easy blue and green runs. Half the runs on this second, or "back" face of the mountain drop down into a long valley served by Olympia lift; while the other half tend to curve down and around to the right, funneling skiers into a wide flat area with a large warming hut/restaurant complex called the Snoasis.

Behind Snoasis rises a sort of overgrown hill (or mini-mountain), served by two short lifts from opposite sides, and offering short runs of all difficulty. You can ski here, or cross over this mini summit, in order to reach the last skiing zone, Vasquez Ridge. (In fact, you can reach Vasquez Ridge by skiing down below Olympia lift too.) Vasquez is a long low-angle ridge that offers mainly easy blue runs and is served by a monster detachable quad, the Pioneer Express Lift. The skiing on Vasquez Ridge is friendly, unchallenging and uncrowded, but it's a

major undertaking to get back to the main Winter Park areas via the long
Olympia lift. Obviously learners, and less experienced skiers, will find
the backside of Winter Park more to their liking; dyed-in-the-wool
experts will head right for Mary Jane, and skiers in-between (the majority) can find some runs to their liking almost everywhere on this twin
mountain. Let's consider these options in more detail.

WINTER PARK FOR INEXPERIENCED SKIERS

You'll definitely want to avoid Mary Jane your first day at Winter
Park, although once you start finding your way around the mountain and
you're sure you feel comfortable on all the green runs and some of the
easier blue trails, there is one Mary Jane adventure that I'm going to
recommend to you. But for starters, try this sequence. Take any of the
three lower, shorter lifts from the main base (Arrow, Hughes, or Gemini
chairs). Not all of them will be running, unless it's a crowded weekend;
they all arrive at roughly the same spot and, please, don't ask me why
they installed three lifts, almost side by side, going to the same place.
Then warm up on a friendly green trail, *Parkway*, just to get your ski
legs back. Avoid Interstate which is marked on the trail map as the
"easiest way down." It's altogether too roundabout and too flat to enjoy
unless you're a rank beginner. If your first run seems comfortable, take
right off for the top via the lefthand base lift, the Zephyr chair. And
don't get psyched out by the steeper runs you ride over in this chair. All
your skiing will take place on the very friendly backside.

From the top of this lift – a rendezvous known as Sunspot where
several other lifts also arrive – head straight back a hundred yards or so
and turn right down a blue run called *Cranmer* or go a little further, past
a line of trees separating these runs, and take the next run, a green trail
called *Allan Phipps*. At first, everything on this side of the mountain
seems almost the same. As you head down, the runs on the right
steepen, those on your left remain flatter. Take your choice. Take your
choice also whether to contour right around the mountain, following
Allan Phipps, or keep on going more-or-less straight down to Olympia
Lift on *March Hare* or *Mad Tea Party*. Olympia lift generally offers the
best skiing at Winter Park for strong novices or weaker, less experienced
intermediates, so you'll get to know it pretty well.

Two other options will help inexperienced skiers stave off the
boredom of always remaining on one part of the mountain. You can ski
down to the Pioneer Express quad, and ski on Vasquez Ridge by sticking
to *Gunbarrel* and *Lonesome Whistle*. But remember that the blue runs
on Vasquez Ridge tend to be more difficult and demanding than the blue

runs on Olympia lift. There's also the Mary Jane adventure I promised: From the top of Mary Jane (reached either by the Summit Express lift from the Mary Jane base, or by the High Lonesome lift) you'll find several very long, very easy, but very scenic green routes to take you back down to the Winter Park side. (The best of these is *Switchyard*.) There's definitely enough easy skiing at Winter Park to give even timid skiers a sense of exploring a big mountain.

WINTER PARK FOR AVERAGE SKIERS

You're a good solid intermediate: what to expect? where to go? There are so many runs, aimed in so many different directions, that it's all too easy to waste hours of your skiing day zigzagging around the mountain with no game plan, getting stuck on a lot of the boring, road-like connectors that abound at Winter Park. My recommendation to strong but not overly bold or ambitious skiers (skiers who don't want to spend all day boogying and bashing in the bumps) is this: You'll find the most enjoyable upper intermediate skiing on the two extreme sides of the mountain. That is to say, on the far side of Vasquez Ridge and on the farther backside slopes of Mary Jane. Generally, you can ignore the blue slopes of the main or middle section of Winter Park because, frankly, they lack character and interest. Don't worry, you'll get to see this part of the mountain anyway, cruising down *Jabberwocky* or *White Rabbit* on your way from Lunch Rock (the name of the Mary Jane summit) back down to the Vasquez side; it's just not worth tarrying here.

The blue runs on Vasquez Ridge, like *Stagecoach*, *Sundance* and *Quickdraw*, have plenty of character. They twist and turn; their pitch and contour change often; their steeps flatten out before they can psych you out; and when moguls appear, they do so in inviting patches rather than forbidding phalanxes. The only flaw with skiing over here – as on any long ridge – is that when runs follows a natural fall line down the flank of the ridge, they always bottom out too soon. So you'll wind up with a few boring minutes of flat skiing along *Big Valley* or *Wagon Train* at the end of every good run on Vasquez Ridge.

In fact, even without a degree in ski-area design, it will strike you that the bottom terminal of the quad lift that serves Vasquez Ridge has been placed a few hundred yards too low, because these last few hundred yards seem to be pointless, flat, skating terrain. Rest assured, there was a reason. The bottom of the Pioneer Express lift is placed in this unlikely spot in order to let it link up with future lifts and runs that will someday open up all of the Vasquez drainage, right up to those pure white corniced bowls you can see in the distance. Patience!...

The backside of Mary Jane has a pleasant surprise in store for good skiers: real open-glade skiing through a naturally thinned out high-altitude forest in *Wildwood Glade* and *Bellmar Bowl*. This is a special treat at Winter Park, because most of the forests on the mountain are so dense and dark that they're almost oppressive. This open top area on the backside of Mary Jane also offers the best views on the mountain. A sweeping panorama up to the big peaks on the continental divide rather than the endless succession of green timbered slopes one gazes at (and soon comes to ignore) on the front side. Although not at all challenging, I find these runs, along with *Roundhouse*, to be among the most esthetic experiences at Winter Park. The new Sunnyside triple chair, up the backside of Mary Jane, has made these runs even more attractive by sparing skiers a long slow comeback trail

It's also a good place for intermediate skiers to push their skill and comfort levels upwards, one notch at a time, without risking any un-pleasant surprises. If you're a pretty fair skier, who wants to start challenging steeper and bumpier slopes, you should take advantage of several trails marked with an alternating blue-and-black line on the trail map. These are perfect transition runs to test yourself on, before attack-ing the real black diamonds. On the Mary Jane side, ski *Sleeper* before trying any of the black runs. And on the main "front" face at Winter Park, try *Hughes* or *Bradley's Bash* (a smidgen harder) before tackling any blacks.

Winter Park is definitely not one of those obvious-to-ski areas like Copper Mountain where a trail map seems almost redundant and skiers couldn't get lost if they tried. But one of the advantages of skiing a complicated mountain is that if you keep your wits about you, you can find slopes of virtually any difficulty on any exposure. My hints should keep you on the right track until you've found your own favorites.

WINTER PARK FOR VERY STRONG SKIERS

There are ski mountains in Colorado where the three-color, national trail marking system has been skewed so far, one way or the other, that skiers can look at a blue square or black diamond sign and still not have a clue as to what sort experience awaits them, what sort of terrors, or delights. When I skied and reskied every area in Colorado, gathering info for this book, I found one area calling a slope blue that could have been "double black" anywhere else; and other areas where the black slopes were ridiculously easy. I tell you this so you'll know it's a complement when I say that Winter Park's rating system is very honest. If a trail is marked black, it is. That means two things: it's steep and

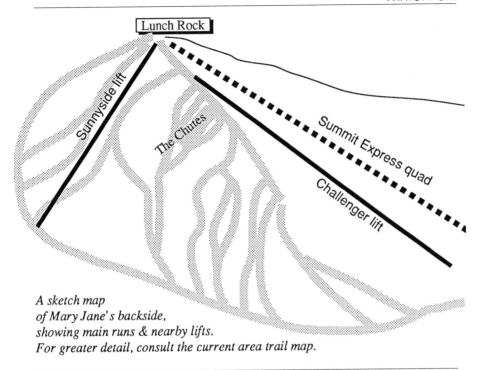

Lunch Rock

Sunnyside lift

The Chutes

Summit Express quad

Challenger lift

A sketch map
of Mary Jane's backside,
showing main runs & nearby lifts.
For greater detail, consult the current area trail map.

there'll be plenty of bumps. Winter Park's black runs are not wimpy.

But they're not ugly either. I find the bumps on Mary Jane unusually well formed, big and rhythmic with rounded exit gullies. Seemingly these bumps don't get hacked up and chopped off, because skiers here avoid such runs if they are not ready for them. But you are. Bravo! The gullies and short cliff-like walls of upper section of Mary Jane, around *Sluice Box* and *Pine Cliffs*, are good warm ups before tackling the harder bump lines to your right (looking down). The dividing line between the front and back sides of Mary Jane is a long bumped-out ridge run called *Derailer*, and the hardest, best bump runs come off it on both sides. I find the backside runs like *Cannonball* and *Long* and *Short Haul* to be straighter, steeper and more continuous than the bump runs on the other side — more fun too, once you're into it.

The most difficult and certainly the most exciting runs in all Winter Park are the three chutes, *Awe Chute*, *Baldy's Chute* and *Jeff's Chute*, that drop off the backside of the *Derailer* ridge. They are reached via a special gate on the side of Derailer, furnished with a special and very sobering warning sign. If the conditions aren't adequate, that is to say, not enough snow or too hard or icy, the patrol closes this gate. Take these runs very seriously. They are very steep, narrow, twisty and rocky; and a fall could be dangerous. It's a tribute to the spirit of Winter Park management that these runs are marked and often open. As long as skiers can continue to find challenges like this at ski areas, downhill skiing still qualifies as an adventure sport.

BASE FACILITIES & VILLAGE.

The trail map tells you that the big base facility at the bottom of the main mountain is called "The Village at Winter Park." Why not? It's a big interesting place, full of shops and eateries, and actually more interesting than the town of Winter Park a few miles down the road. There's the rub. You can call it a town, but it doesn't feel like one. It certainly doesn't feel like a Colorado ski town. And this town, or absence of town, is the big flaw in Winter Park's winter offering.

The town of Winter Park is an unplanned, underdeveloped strip of a town, a lose collection of random access parking lots and shopping, eating and lodging facilities thrown up in the woods on either side of US 40 for a couple of miles. One of those less-than urban assemblies where the individual elements may work (for example, there are a couple of wonderful old 1940's style dark wooden lodges, and a couple of really handsome contemporary condo castles) but where nothing is tied to anything else, where there's no center, no circulation, no local character. Too bad. Reminds me of Mammoth Lakes, California, another non-starter in the mountain village sweepstakes, where uncontrolled strip development provided a lot of lodging units but knocked out any chance of real resort town life. Enough said.

Is it too late? I don't know. It's easy enough to see why a proper town didn't develop here. For years and years Winter Park was the classic popular weekend destination for Denver skiers and little more. After a remarkable period of ski area expansion, Winter Park's mountain facilities are on a par with Colorado's other destination resorts. Maybe a hot ski town can grow out of the chaos down the road, I hope so.

The ski area base itself is an interesting hodgepodge of architecture, skier services and good vibes. The entrance buildings, ticket windows, etc. are intact monuments to ski history, with a building style that could be called early Forest Service Tyrolean. Just beyond, rises an impressive cubist structure of corrugated metal and glass, an integrated mini-mall of retail, rental, eating and drinking spots, that really works. There are sun decks facing the mountain everywhere, and a classic, timeless apres-ski scene with collegiate overtones of beer drinking and girl watching is well underway here long before the lifts close.

WINTER PARK DATA

KEY PHONE NUMBERS

Snow Conditions	(303) 666-4502 (Denver Metro)
Area Information	(303) 726-5514
	(303) 892-0961 (Denver)
Central Reservations	1-800-453-2525
also	(303) 447-0588 (Denver Metro)
also	(303) 726-5587 (in state)

TRANSPORTATION

By car, 1 1/2 hour drive (in good road and weather conditions) from Denver on I-70 to exit 232 (7 miles west of Idaho Springs) and then west on U.S. 40.

By bus from Stapleton Airport; also Gray Line daily from Denver

By plane to Stapleton Airport in Denver.

By train, daily scheduled service from San Francisco east and Chicago west on the California Zepher; also Rio Grande Ski Train weekend service from Denver (leaves Denver's Union Station at 7:30 A.M, direct to Winter Park's slopes; leaves Winter Park at 4:00 P.M.) For more information call Amtrak, 1-800-USA-RAIL.

Free Shuttle Bus from nearby town of Fraser, and between Winter Park and Mary Jane.

MOUNTAIN STATISTICS

	Winter Park	*Mary Jane*	*Vasquez Ridge*
Vertical Drop	2,200 feet	1,770 feet	1,214 feet
Summit Elev.	11,220 feet	11,220 feet	10,770 feet
Base Elevation	9,000 feet	9,450 feet	9,486 feet
Skiing Terrain	1,105 acres		
Number of Lifts	19 including 2 high-speed detachable quads		
Uphill Capacity	27,884 skiers per hour		
Snowboarding	Yes		

Bumps or moguls on a ski slope can delight or frustrate. I love them, but most skiers, I know, don't. Which is natural because they have a hard time with them. Not a hard time turning. The reason bumps exist at all is because any little high spot or lump on the slope, serving as a natural pivot point, facilitates turning your skis. Skiers figure this out early, and use bumps (whether they enjoy bump skiing or not) to trigger or launch their turns. The real problem comes in putting it all together, staying in balance on a moguled slope, controlling your speed in the limited space available, and arriving at the end of one bump turn, poised, comfortable and ready for the next. In a word, finishing a bump turn well is harder than starting that turn. Here's a basic plan that should improve your mogul skiing manyfold.

Start your bump turns the way you always do – only less so. I mean by that, when you cross over the top of a bump don't pivot your skis as hard as you normally do. Trust in the fact that your skis will follow the scraped out hollow of the bump's trough. That's right, the round shape of the turn is already there, in the rounded shape of the bump's gully; and all you need to do is let your skis drift. They will follow the curved gully in an arc that brings you around under the bump.

Most skiers who have trouble with bumps simply overpivot their skis on the very top. They complete the entire turning action in the first foot or two, and find themselves out of balance with their skis jammed sideways, crosswise to the gully at its narrowest point. One reason that skiers seem to have a hard time, just letting their skis drift on down through the gully, is anxiety about picking up too much speed. It's true, you will go a little faster right in the middle of each turn, as you're coming around the side of the bump. But you will finish each turn underneath the bump, where you'll have more room to turn your skis sideways without getting them caught in the gully.

I can't promise that there will always be a lot of room under every bump; but there will certainly be more room below the bump than in the gully beside it. So your basic pattern for comfortable bump skiing is: a slow start, pivoting your skis just enough to get them started; a relaxed middle phase drifting around the bump, letting your skis follow the rounded gully; and finally, an active finish below the bump where you

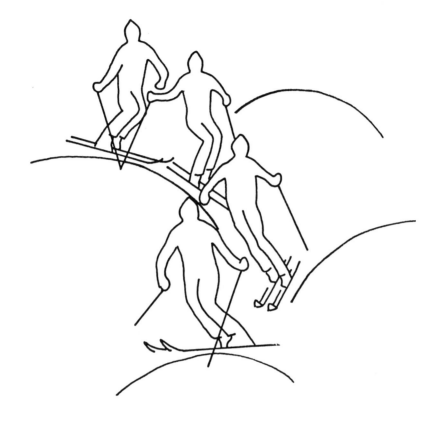

actually turn your skis as far across the slope as you want to slow down.
Remember, slow down beneath the bump, not in the middle.

Another tip: Use your pole to banish hesitation in bumps. If you
reach from turn to turn with your outside pole, extending it straight
down the hill toward the next bump and stabbing that bump decisively,
then you'll probably turn on time. A decisive pole plant doesn't guarantee a good turn, but it will trigger a turning response rather than letting
you hesitate, freeze, and skitter off in an awkward traverse through a
mine field of moguls. Avoid traverses. In bumps more than anywhere
else, "one good turn deserves another."

CHAPTER 8   LOVELAND

This is the one that almost didn't make it into my *Insider's Guide.* I blush to tell you why. The truth is that although I had driven by this small ski area, nestled under (and spreading out above) the East Portal of the Eisenhower Tunnel on Interstate 70 dozens, no, probably hundreds of times since I moved to Colorado in 1976, I was just too snobbish to stop and ski there—until recently. Better just drive on through the tunnel, I always thought, into Summit County, or if the roads were good, turn off I-70 and drive over Loveland Pass to Arapahoe Basin, another small area but one that always seemed more imposing, more alpine... How could such a small area as Loveland offer good, serious, exciting skiing? I was dead wrong. I'm glad to admit it.

Loveland is tiny, the smallest ski area in this guide book. And in fact, it's precisely that, a ski *area*, a day area, and not at all a true ski *resort* in the normal Colorado sense of the term. But it's a real gem. An area that offers some stunning skiing, as well as a type of ski experience that's hard to find elsewhere. Loveland is no grand success story as a ski area, and one gets the feeling that it's been left behind in the white revolution that's been transforming Colorado skiing into something resembling a brand new sport. It seems half deserted on weekdays, and even on weekends, when the parking lot finally fills up, mostly with Denver skiers since this is the closest area to Denver, Loveland still doesn't seem full or crowded. Except for a couple of new triple chairs, the lifts are old, double chairs, and they are all painted a shade of powder blue that somehow makes them look older than they are. A newly renovated base lodge is about their only concession to progress. I'd say; and the whole Loveland experience seems to come straight out of another place, another time. For one thing, the daily skiing ticket is wonderfully cheap. For another, in this age of heightened ski-area liability concerns and general corporate up-tightness, there are even places at Loveland where the ski area boundary is left vague, almost undefined. Where the distinction between tamed ski area and still wild mountainscape is no longer clear. And this is exactly what I like about Loveland skiing.

THE LAYOUT AND FEEL OF THE MOUNTAIN

Strike that word "mountain." Loveland is a bowl or high alpine basin rather than a peak. It's set amongst mountains to be sure, the high summits and ridges of the Continental Divide. Its main base area is only a stone's throw from the twin tunnels where Interstate 70 plunges under these peaks en route from Denver to Dillon, Vail, ultimately to Grand Junction and points west. And even from the highway you can see that just above this base, above the tunnel, everything changes.

Timberline is only a few hundred feet above the parking lot; the dense front-range forest thins out quickly and disappears altogether in a last scattering of sparse, stunted, dwarf trees. The world turns white or almost white: snowy basins and distant corniced ridges alternate with windswept rock, patchy cliffs. In its openness, Loveland is the exact antithesis of the last area we visited, Winter Park, which has been literally chopped out of deep dense forested slopes, where every run is bounded by curtains of dark green. Here the eye ranges unchecked across wide and wide-open snow basins: an alpine rather than sub-alpine world. An unmistakable, high-mountain feeling infects Loveland skiing.

For the most part, Loveland skiing isn't very hard. The ski area has two parts: Loveland Basin, spread out above the freeway tunnel is, for me, the real ski area. And there is also a mysterious appendage about a mile down the road, called Loveland Valley, which has a tiny beginners chair and a medium-sized double chair serving a couple of blue runs. The two halves of the area are linked by a long *horizontal* chairlift (lift 5) that exists only to shuttle skiers back and forth. Don't bother, stay up on top.

The main area has only four chair lifts and one poma, fanning out in a semi-circle into all sides of the basin above the highway. The leftmost chair (looking up) is the steepest, and serves respectable, even fierce black bump runs, as well as a number of interesting blues that sweep around into the center of the basin rather than descending the steep face above the lodge. While this triple chair (lift 1) serves the most technically demanding runs at Loveland, this is not where you'll find the most beautiful skiing. And in fact this side of the basin has the thickest densest trees, so it doesn't share in that high, above-timberline atmosphere I mentioned earlier.

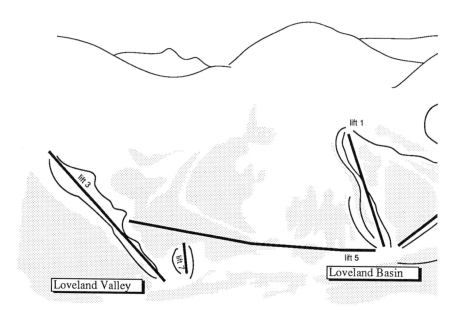

To get right into the Loveland feeling, take chair 2, another triple, up to the area's highest unloading ramp (at 12,230 ft.), and you'll find your self in the middle of a big expansive bowl that seems to invite you to ski in all directions at once. Which is just what you do.... What I mean is that, although the named "runs" or "lines" indicated on the trail map up here are all easy-angled blues and a few greens, there are no boundaries between them. Or anywhere up here. You are quickly tempted into a more dashing free-form style of skiing, big-turn cruising, where you look for mountain shapes to turn on, rather than just repeating your same old moves down the middle of a well defined run. The stunted, tree-line vegetation (often resembling evergreen bushes more than mini-trees) gives you widely spaced points of green to turn around. There are friendly rolls, dips and gullies that all lend themselves to flowing, smooth, high-speed skiing.

Just beside the top of chair 2, you'll see a wooden chalet-like structure. Ah ha, you think, a snack bar or top-of-the-mountain restaurant. Nope, it's a picnic hut called Ptarmigan Roost. Just the idea of a

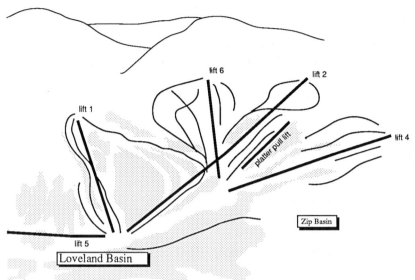

*A sketch map of
Loveland Basin & Valley,
showing lifts and main runs. For greater
detail consult the current area trail map which is
larger and indicates the names and difficulty of all runs.
(Please note that the above maps overlap in the center areas.)*

ski area not exploiting this spot and leaving the hut for those who pack
their lunch in a rucksack takes you back to an earlier, more romantic era.
I love it. You want to dash down to the base, buy lunch in the cafeteria
or a hamburger at the outdoor grill and take it up the lift with you to
enjoy, along with the view, from this old-time warming hut. Do it.

From the top of chair 2, you'll find you can travel and explore a long
way to the right or left, into and through a number of other sub-basins,
served by three other lifts. You'll explore without keeping score because, to tell the truth, the different runs up here all tend to blur together
but not from boredom. After an hour you can't tell them apart, which is
just fine because they are quite arbitrary in the first place. For me, the
real pleasure at Loveland is that sense of not being bounded or hemmed
in by any particular run. Heading in any direction I please and knowing
it's okay: just over that roll, on the other side of that boulder, beyond
that tiny grove of trees, there'll be more open friendly open slopes
waiting. It doesn't feel like typical Colorado skiing. *Vive la difference!*

IN BOUNDS, OUT OF BOUNDS

But what really won me over to Loveland was the skiing in *Zip Basin*. This is the farthest righthand aspect of the basin, looking up from below. Zip Basin is wonderfully indistinct on the trail map, even more so when you complete a long leftward traverse from the top of chair 4, actually going round the shoulder of a peak, turning the corner, to come out at the top of a long series of open slopes. They drop away leftward into a sort of gully or natural drain, way down there below you. Surprise: you've skied clear out of sight of the ski area behind you (although you can still look across the basin to the tiny bumps off there on chair 1); and most of the time, you and your friends will be the only skiers around. Zip Basin is a sort of secret preserve of unpacked snow which few skiers bother with even though it's on the map. Very much a miniature sort of Back Bowls experience, compared to Vail for example, but how often do you get the Back Bowl at Vail all to yourself? Never.

There are a loft of different lines to ski back here. The slopes are continuous, never very steep, and sometimes the snow is windblown enough to be a real challenge. It's not at all clear where the ski area stops out here in Zip Basin, and it doesn't seem to matter because any line you ski here will funnel you down into the natural drainage of a side valley slanting back down toward the I-70 freeway and the ski area base. The few tracks you encounter back here in *Zip Basin* eventually merge into a sort of trail that snakes down the creek-bed drainage (this is what's marked *Zip Trail* on the map) and finishes above the highway on a steeper shoulder that's usually moguled.

There's only one puzzle left: how to get back to the ski area, which is over there, on the other side of a four-lane interstate highway? It's not really a mystery. Ski tracks will lead you rightwards toward a tiny cement pedestrian tunnel that crosses under the freeway and brings one back to the Loveland base lodge. Not bad. I chuckled to think of all the times I had driven unsuspecting over this spot, unaware that accommodating highway engineers had constructed a comeback route for skiers who have just enjoyed one of the best hidden runs in Colorado! You come out too low to simply hop on chair 4 and do it again. But the fact that you have to take two lifts to get back up there, plus the fact that this skiing is mostly out-of-sight from anywhere, should help keep *Zip Basin* such an underused, well preserved, in-bounds out-of-bounds experience.

LOVELAND DATA

KEY PHONE NUMBERS

Snow Conditions	(303) 569-2288
Ski Area Information	(303) 571-5580 (from Denver)

TRANSPORTATION

By car, 55 minute drive (in good road and weather conditions) from Denver on I-70 to Exit 216 just before the Eisenhower Tunnel.

MOUNTAIN STATISTICS

Vertical Drop	1,430 feet
Summit Elev.	12,230 feet
Base Elevation	10,800 feet
Skiing Terrain	686 acres
Longest Run	1 1/2 miles
Number of Lifts	8 including 2 surface lifts
Uphill Capacity	9,000 per hour
Snowboarding	Yes

"Off piste," a wonderful expression, a wonderful feeling. European skiers, who call their ski runs "pistes," use this expression to describe skiing away from prepared runs. Not just powder skiing but skiing in a mixed bag of variable, natural snow conditions. Skiing that demands an adaptable and secure technique to cope with anything from wind-ruffled powder to breakable crust. Zip Basin at Loveland, an area exposed to sun and wind and seldom completely ski-packed, is a perfect spot to experience the delights and frustrations of unprepared, variable snow. Here are a few general tips and strategies to use whenever you ski in tricky variable snow conditions:

Security first. Maybe the surface will support you, maybe it won't, but if you have doubts, then ski it slowly; high-speed tumbles are much riskier. And ski it on two feet, both skis equally weighted. This is the opposite of normal packed-slope technique where you want to be exclusively in balance over your outside ski. But in "unknown" snow conditions, equal weighting gives you several advantages. If the snow surface has a light unstable crust, you're less likely to break through with only half the weight on each ski. And if one ski does break through to become trapped inside or under the crust, then you've still got your other ski for support and turning while you try to get it (i.e. them) back together.

For similar reasons, I suggest medium radius turns in variable and tricky snow conditions. Short radius turns can be so violent that your likely to break through the crusty top layers and get caught, while long-radius turns tend to build up too much speed, too quickly.

If the snow seems extremely variable and "catchy," you'll probably want to use a smooth powerful up motion to start your turns. Add that snappy lifting of your outside hand and arm (that I mentioned in connection with powder) to punctuate this up movement. But don't simply jump in the air, turn your skis and come down hard. This hard landing can wipe out all the advantage of a smooth powerful up unweighting by trapping your skis again in deep crusty snow. Instead try to follow your smooth upward extension with an equally smooth progressive sinking, to absorb some of the extra pressure of this "landing."

In difficult variable snow I make an unabashed effort to lean or bank

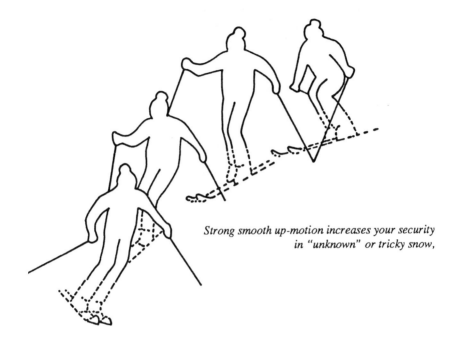

*Strong smooth up-motion increases your security
in "unknown" or tricky snow,*

*into my turns. This tilts your skis up in the snow, reducing the likelihood
of catching an outside edge in the crust. Not something I'd ever recommend on a packed slope, but a helpful factor in heavy difficult snow.*

   *Of course, skiing off-piste doesn't necessarily mean you'll encounter
difficult snow. Sometimes it's perfect white velvet out there. The idea is
simply to be conservative for the first couple of turns and if the snow
turns out to be uniform and easy then just relax and let 'em rip. I'll
often use a preturn, or slight uphill christy, just before launching a turn
down the hill as a means of testing, or previewing the snow conditions.
But remember, your biggest safety factor in variable unknown snow is to
weight both skis equally.*

PART IV

THE SUMMIT

CHAPTER 9   KEYSTONE

Keystone is a fabulous success story in Colorado skiing, the little ski area that could. Keystone is hardly little any more – quite the contrary – and has been beautifully organized, developed and expanded to a degree no one except the visionaries who did it would have believed possible a decade ago. It's tempting to say that Bob Maynard and his team, who took over Keystone's destiny when the Ralston Purina corporation bought the original wee ski area, made a silk purse out of a sow's ear. But that's not exactly fair. It is fair, however, to say that Keystone is not a great natural ski mountain, being a bit short of both natural snowfall and ideal skiing terrain, especially open terrain. Like Winter Park, this is a densely forested dark green mountain. Even the Keystone trail map, which after all is only an idealized artist's conception that can really convey any desired impression, looks a good deal greener than that of other mountains (and I'm talking green forests, not "green" runs). But Keystone has been cut, carved, groomed and polished into one of the biggest, most successful ski areas in the state. They have consistently broken new ground in skier service here, starting with Colorado's first giant modern snowmaking system. And it's paid off because Keystone is a perennial favorite with Denver skiers, who have the opportunity in one winter to sample more Colorado ski areas than most out-of-state skiers can visit in five years.

Keystone is two areas in one, and maybe more if you want to count the artificially lit night-skiing runs separately. Still more if you count its older, smaller and higher cousin, Arapahoe Basin, which is run by the same company with the same polish. However, I'm giving A-Basin a chapter of its own. There's the main mountain at Keystone, a big, broad flank of forest-lined fairways, groomed sweeps that flow rather than drop toward the valley: smooth, fast and relaxed trail skiing. And then there's North Peak, the mountain behind the mountain: a recent addition with new lifts, new exposures, new views, and generally more difficult and challenging skiing than that found on the front side. Just as in the case of Winter Park's Mary Jane, there has been an attempt to market North Peak as a separate ski venue, complete with its own lighting-bolt logo, its own mystique. Chalk that one up to pure PR. North Peak is simply a terrific addition to a mountain that was previously too heavily weighted toward novice and low intermediate skiers; it balances the spectrum at the upper end.

And there's also a village. A small but very attractive modern resort village that, like Keystone's mountain, is more a triumph of hard work and try-harder management than of natural advantages. The problem is simply that Keystone's resort village isn't at the base of the ski mountain but a couple of miles down the road. By the time serious resort planning began at Keystone, the land at the base of the ski mountain was lost in a hodgepodge of individual ownership and speculation. Today, the lovely valley below the ski area is slowly filling in with a most unlovely mix of condos and fragmented shopping centers that would be more in place in Denver suburbs than in the mountains. Down the road, however, Keystone village is esthetically pleasing, tightly integrated, and altogether successful. It's a true pedestrian precinct that spreads (but doesn't sprawl) around an artificial lake, which in winter turns into Colorado's finest outdoor skating spot. Nicely done. We'll take a second look after our tour of the mountain.

THE SHAPE AND FEEL OF KEYSTONE MOUNTAIN

Keystone is a wide ski mountain, as wide or wider side to side as it is tall. This impression is reinforced by the fact that the mountain has two base locations. On the western side, closer to Keystone Village, the original base is focused around an attractive day lodge called the Mountain House. While further up the canyon, there is a separate parking complex (big lots checkerboarded among trees) that serves Keystone's high-speed Skyway gondola. The Gondola takes you from the River Run Plaza to the Summit House in one straight shot, and is the only real high-speed lift on the mountain.

Despite its twin base areas, the Keystone mountain divides neatly in thirds. The Gondola and the Erickson chair, define and serve the east side; then there's what I think of as the center or middle mountain, served by the Argentine lift from the Mountain House base and three higher chairs, Montezuma, Saints John and Ida Belle; and finally the western side of Keystone mountain, served by the Peru and the two Packsaddle lifts. (All the lifts here, you may already have guessed, are

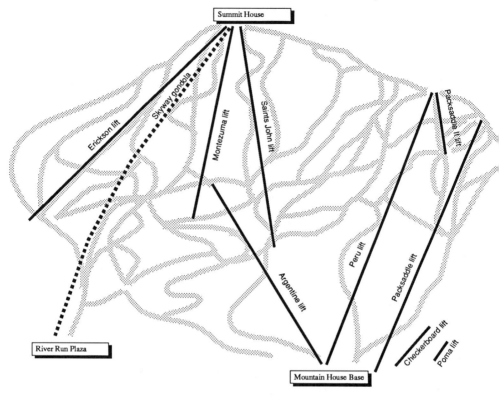

A sketch map of the front face of Keystone Mountain.
For greater detail, always check a current ski area trail map.

named after historic mine sites.)

I find this far western side of the mountain to have more character than the rest of the front face. Not necessarily better skiing, but more distinctive skiing, because on a big forested mountain like Keystone runs can begin to resemble one another; and there's a remarkable similarity among the long blue runs on the center mountain. It's hard sometimes for non-locals to tell runs like *Flying Dutchman, Frenchman* and *Paymaster* apart. Whereas on the western side, one starts with *Packsaddle Bowl*, Keystone's only real open-slope skiing and a delightful contrast to its tree-lined roller coasters. This is a great place to head early in the morning, because *Packsaddle Bowl* is tilted somewhat east to catch the early sun. Then, proceeding down this far western flank, you encounter some serious black slopes, the hardest skiing on the front mountain — and you know you're not just cruising another Keystone ski boulevard.

KEYSTONE STYLE, KEYSTONE SNOW

Keystone is a good cruising mountain and Keystone skiers figure out right away that on a mountain this friendly, speed adds excitement. The average Keystone skier is nowhere near as skilled as Aspen skiers, nowhere near as well dressed as Vail skiers, but I'm always struck by how gutsy skiers here are. There's a go-for-it attitude in the air, and Keystone skiers, even inexperienced novices, are simply not timid. And there's also an intriguing relation between skiing style and snow surface here.

Keystone is both the pioneer and the acknowledged leader among Colorado resorts when it comes to artificial snow. Today the whole front face of the mountain is 100% covered by the snowmaking system. Not that Colorado snow is that unpredictable, or sparse – but the truth is that no ski area in the world can guarantee good skiing conditions in November and December every year. Snowmaking alters the flip-of-the-coin uncertainty in early season vacation planning, and at Keystone the early season (sometimes from mid October on) is always safe. They not only make a lot of early snow, they groom the daylights out of it. Which is crucial because if left untended, artificial snow turns to ice. At its best it's still a hard surface and the only way to make such hard snow agreeable is to throw a lot of money, manpower and machinery at it: tilling, raking, scraping, texturing, churning up the surface with "powder makers" and other hydraulic gizmos that sprout from modern snow cats like ray guns from space vehicles in a George Lucas film. Keystone does a very good job of keeping its artificial snow in good shape. And this constant grooming and snow care means that you can just forget moguls on the front face, there aren't any. Which is one reason skiers like to move fast here. Also the snowfall in this end of Summit County is steady but comes in small doses rather than big dumps; and what happens is that fast-skiing intermediate skiers, who skid most of their turns are forever scraping the new snow off to the sides of the runs. In short, the smooth hard snow encourages a fast skidded style of skiing, and this style in turn helps keep the snow smooth, scrapped and hard. At Keystone, the rather hard artificial-snow surface tends to persist all season. A rarity in Colorado.

Such snow would be a definite minus for Keystone skiing, if the mountain weren't so accommodating, gracious and well managed. Despite the consistently hard, scraped snow, this is always a pleasant mountain to visit. And of course, it's a trade off. In return, skiers have a longer, earlier season, and on occasional dry years, a better one. But that's only the front of the mountain.

NORTH PEAK

To reach North Peak, the other half of the Keystone experience, you ski down one of two trails from the top of Keystone mountain (the Summit House at 11,660 feet). And so doing, enter a different world. North Peak really is a another, separate forested peak behind the main mountain: here too trails are cut not natural, but they are a good deal steeper, a good deal more stimulating for advanced skiers. A number of runs back here are also equipped with snowmaking but the snow never has that scraped, front-side feeling, in large part because the style of skiing changes back here: turns shorten, the terrain demands a more conscious, more curvy, less straight-ahead style.

Diamond Back, one of the two runs that take you down to North Peak, is a river of black bumps that has a funny sun exposure, which means it's seldom good skiing till afternoon. The other, a blue beauty called *Mozart*, is the finest run at Keystone, at least for me. It feels spacious, inviting, and extremely varied: random tree islands block then reveal views; the terrain is constantly folding and rippling into small micro-gullies, drops, momentary sidehills. An irresistible invitation to playful skiing. *Mozart*, a great name for a great run.

On North Peak itself, served by the Santiago triple chair, you have your choice of mostly bumped out black and blue runs. But surprise: for those skiers who don't yet feel at home in bumps, these are the friendliest mogul runs in Colorado (well actually there are a couple of similar runs at Steamboat, but you'll find more user-friendly bumps here.) What makes these bumps easy to ski? Steady sustained pitches rather than drops and flats. And perhaps also, the fact that two categories of skiers are conspicuously absent here: inexperienced skiers who wander onto bump runs by accident and chop off the backsides of bumps with panic pivots; and equally destructive, the real hot shots who ski straighter faster lines and hammer rounded gullies into narrow slots with the tails of their skis. As an instructor, my eyes light up when I ski North Peak runs. This is just the sort of inviting bump terrain I would choose to introduce good skiers to the esoteric pleasures of mogul skiing. You'll usually find one or two bumpless runs back here that have been recently groomed, but generally North Peak is all bump skiing, albeit of a pleasant, almost relaxing variety. Don't miss it.

SPEAKING OF LEARNING

My overall impression is that the ski school at Keystone is one of the best in Colorado. Partly because they've had some very good direction and leadership over the years. But above all because of the

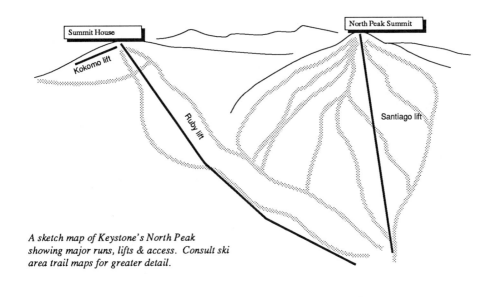

A sketch map of Keystone's North Peak showing major runs, lifts & access. Consult ski area trail maps for greater detail.

enormous number of students and lessons on this mountain. Nothing teaches ski instructors how to teach like teaching itself. And Keystone instructors are busy enough to learn an awful lot.

I don't think you've had to read between the lines here to discover that I don't consider Keystone a challenging or exciting mountain for expert skiers — but then, most skiers aren't experts. Keystone is a friendly, accessible mountain, where new skiers can quickly ski down from the very top and have a great time. In fact, it's an ideal "learning mountain." Couple the friendly inviting terrain with the depth of ski school experience that I already mentioned, and you've got one of the best spots in Colorado for less experienced skiers to take lessons.

KEYSTONE BY NIGHT

Night skiing is well known in some parts of the country – in the East and Midwest it's an accepted way for urban ski hordes to get maximum benefit from small nearby areas — but Keystone is the only major area in Colorado to offer night skiing. And like everything else they've done, they've done it well. The gondola is the main route up at night, although the Argentine lift also runs, providing beginner access to some gentle green trails. Some 13 runs are well lit. If you're spending a week in Summit County, this is definitely worth one night just for the change of scene. Make it a full night out with a fondue dinner in the Summit House, at *der Fondue Chessel*, a sort of improvised restaurant created nightly out of daytime cafeteria space on top of the mountain, complete with Tyrolean band and yodel singers. Sound corny? It is; but somehow it works. And when dinner is followed by long eerie runs in the iridescent purple shadows cast by high vapor lamps, under a tent of high-altitude stars, on a ball-bearing carpet of moon gray snow – well, you've got all the ingredients of an unforgettable, surrealistic evening.

KEYSTONE VILLAGE TIPS

Skating on the frozen lake is a must. It too is lit at night, and rental skates are available. Probably the best Keystone dinner is at The Ranch, a refurbished log cabin on the nearby golf course. But an even more romantic place to dine is not in Keystone itself but ten minutes drive away, up Montezuma Road toward the old ghost town of Montezuma. I mean Ski Tip Ranch, a wood and plaster, Austro-alpine hideaway hand-built among dense aspen stands by Max Dercum, who started Keystone. The Dercum family has sold Ski Tip but the romance lives on; it's a lovely inn too, but you don't have to stay at Ski Tip to dine there. And the best breakfast spot in Keystone village is the Edgewater.

But to tell the truth, as attractive as I find this village development at Keystone – clean unpretentious architecture, stepped down the hillside from a wonderfully bold concrete and glass main lodge, with a series of pedestrian walks and plazas, and dramatic views over the skating lake toward the ski mountain – it just isn't big enough, active enough or diverse enough to keep you interested for a whole week.

Of course, in Summit County that isn't a tragedy. From Keystone you're a short drive away from three other serious ski mountains, two of which have their own base-area/village complexes. Even nearer, there's the Dillon/Silverthorne area, the rambling high-altitude suburbs around Lake Dillon, just off the I-70 Interstate, which one drives through en route to Keystone. Even though Keystone Village is the nicest place to stay in this east end of Summit County, a lot of Keystone skiers stay in and around Dillon, and save money by doing it.

There are also several good restaurants in the Dillon area, of which the best is the Ristorante del Lago in nearby Silverthorne. And there is at least one all-time classic, a barn-like Mexican restaurant and honky tonk, the Old Dillon Inn, just a block or two the other side of I-70 when you follow the main drag in from Keystone. Generations of ski bums, instructors and lift operators have found happiness in the dark, dense atmosphere of the Dillon Inn. Maybe you will too.

KEYSTONE DATA

KEY PHONE NUMBERS

Snow Conditions   (303) 468-4111
                               (303) 733-0191 (from Denver)

Ski Area Information   1-800-222-0188
                    also   (303) 468-2316

Reservations   1-800-222-0188 (Keystone Condos)
                               1-800-541-0346 (Keystone Lodge)

TRANSPORTATION

By car, 90 minute drive (in good road and weather conditions) from
          Denver on I-70 west through the Eisenhower tunnel to
          the Dillon exit, # 205, then 6 miles east on US high-
          way 6.
By bus or limo, from Denver's Stapleton Airport.

MOUNTAIN STATISTICS

Vertical Drop   2,340 feet
Summit Elev.   11,640 feet
Base Elevation   9,300 feet
Skiing Terrain   680 acres
Number of Lifts   12 including one gondola and 2 surface lifts
Uphill Capacity   13,400 skiers per hour
Snowboarding   No!

Keystone lift tickets are good at Arapahoe Basin. Four and six day Ski
          the Summit passes are available which are good at
          Breckenridge, Copper and Keystone.

It's a matter of regional pride to assert that we never have icy conditions in the Rockies. Of course, it isn't true. But it's certainly fair to say that we have much, much less ice on our slopes than skiers from both coasts are used to. And we certainly experience very "firm" conditions wherever artificial snowmaking systems have been used. Sometimes, as in the case of a World Cup race course, this hard surface is a real advantage; most of the time it's a pain simply because we all ski better on perfect packed powder. Here are a few techniques and tips to help you fight back.

The two main problems that plague skiers on very hard snow are overturning and overedging. The first is natural because a slick hard surface produces so much less friction, that once you twist your skis sideways into a turn, they just keep on turning. Nothing slows down, or inhibits this turning, pivoting action; and before you know it you are skidding sideways in a straight line rather than carving a clean arc. At this point, most skiers compound the problem by trying to "dig in" or edge their skis harder to stop this skidding. It doesn't work. In fact, the harder, or icier, the slope is, the less good it does to strongly edge your skis. Real masters on hard icy snow try to edge their skis just barely enough to hold, knowing that if they overdo it, their skis will immediately start to chatter and slip. So what to do?

Your first step will be to quiet down all your movements, and try to make what I call the minimum start to your turns. That is, just shift to the new ski and wait.... It takes a second for something to happen but this is exactly what you want: a slow, progressive start to the turn, where one weighted ski carves slowly around. If you get impulsive and give one or both skis a powerful twist, then it's all over – you will have initiated a skid, rather than a turn. As long as your skis are primarily slicing forward rather than moving sideways, relatively little edging is required to keep them "on track." But once they've begun to skid out on a very hard, scraped surface, no amount of edging will produce a good turn.

Since the edge of your turning ski doesn't bite or grip the snow very well, the distribution of weight along the edge of that ski becomes critical. If you put too much weight on the front, or on the back of your ski, the tail will break loose in a skid. So it becomes critical to distribute your weight evenly along the whole edge of the carving ski – or, to put it another way, to stand evenly on the edge of that foot, neither on the ball nor on the heel but on the whole foot. One way to maintain this even, unvarying weight distribution is to calm down any upper-body activity, especially arm movement. Spread your arms in a poised balanced position, and keep them there. On icy snow, any sudden arm-hand-pole movement is enough to make your skis skid right out from under you.

And that's your basic strategy for very hard, icy snow: calm almost motionless skiing – as though you were skiing over acres of delicate white eggs, careful not to break a single one with a sudden movement. Try it, it works.

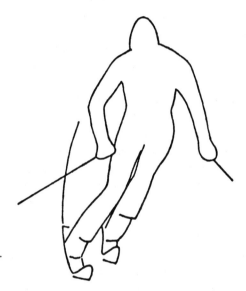

Carving on ice, weight evenly disribted along the edge of the outside ski, body quiet, almost motionless.

CHAPTER 10 ARAPAHOE BASIN

Arapahoe Basin, or "A-Basin" to natives, with a summit elevation of 12,450 feet is the highest ski area in Colorado and one of the oldest. It has the longest season by several months; and it's a real delight. Like Loveland, Arapahoe is one of those small ski areas that feels like a much larger area, precisely because it's set among large and dramatic mountains.

A-Basin is tucked into a kind of fold in the Continental Divide, just over the actual divide on the western side, a few hairpin turns down from the summit of Loveland Pass on what used to be the main road west from Denver. Since the construction of the Eisenhower tunnel, the I-70 Interstate speeds motorists under the Continental Divide into Summit County, and nowadays most skiers get to Arapahoe by driving up the canyon from Keystone (or taking a shuttle bus from Keystone that runs every 20 minutes). You can think of Arapahoe as the older brother, or even the little brother of Keystone. It's owned by the same company, managed in the same flawless style, and shares a common lift ticket with Keystone. But the high alpine flavor of Arapahoe skiing is so different, so special that I wanted to give it a chapter of its own. This is genuine, white on white, above-timberline skiing in a splendid remote setting.

QUICK TOUR OF AN ALPINE AREA

There are only four full-sized chairlifts at A-Basin (plus one wee beginners' lift) but despite this the mountain offers a lot of variety. The main chair up from the base lodge is the Exhibition triple, and both this lift and the runs it serves are still in the forested zone. But above Exhibition lift, the scene changes. The last trees thin and rapidly disappear. Skiers can enjoy every square meter of several wide-open rolling bowls – gullies and faces, humps and hollows, a white playground. This upper area is served by two more lifts, the Norway and Lenawee double chairs; and the skiing up here is marked a sort of generic "blue" (with the exception of one easier angled hollow known as *Dercum's Gulch* after the same Max Dercum who built Ski Tip Ranch and started the Keystone ski area). None of these slopes is really steep; but they are constantly varied and have so much character that no one could be bored. When one skis this sort of treeless terrain, it's always possible to dive into beautiful short steep faces right in the middle of an otherwise easy stretch of mountain, pitches that most skiers might avoid but which you can take advantage of if you wish because everything, literally, is skiable.

But if you're looking for more adrenalin, A-Basin can provide it.

ARAPAHOE ADVENTURES

There are two sorts of adventurous skiing here: untracked off-piste lines on the *East Wall* and breathtakingly pure bump skiing in *Pallavicini* couloir.

The *East Wall* is more or less the whole steep mountain flank that you see off to your right when you look down from the top of the Lenawee lift. It's pretty obvious where the skiing stops and the steeper rocky mountainside continues on toward high craggy ridges that overhang the whole area. This is very impressive, alpine-feeling terrain. To ski the *East Wall* you drop off the top a ways and then start traversing out to your right. The farther and higher you traverse, the more turns you'll log on this intriguing "mixed" terrain. There are rocks to avoid, deep drifted gullies to scope out, and altogether lots of room out there on the *East Wall*. The fact that you have to work/walk for it makes these lines even more delicious. Where the *East Wall* blends back into *Wrangler*, there are often one or more kangaroo jumps that are especially popular in springtime – tracked and body packed by wild-eyed college students in shorts!

The bump skiing mecca lies on the other, western side of the area and the Pallavicini lift is bumper headquarters. Possibly the reputation of *Pallavicini*, the main bump run over here, is a little exaggerated, but that's natural because when you look up at it from the parking lot it seems dead vertical. It is steep but believe me, it's not as steep as it looks from below. In addition to steepness, Pallavicini usually has great shaped bumps. Skiers don't wander onto this run by accident, and those that ski it a lot belong there – hence the well formed bumps. First timers on Pallavicini should find the right side looking down a little more friendly, a little less steep and forbidding to enter at the top. There are a number of other black bump runs in the vicinity, all taking you back down to the same lift. But *Pallavicini* is the granddaddy of them all with the best views, the best bumping.

SEASONAL TIPS, EXTRA DIMENSIONS

I haven't yet told you the most important thing about A-Basin. *Ski there in spring.* Yes, it is open for the whole season, from mid-November on, but in winter it can be deadly cold and windy up here; and skiing on tree-sheltered runs at Keystone is generally a better bet. Unless a big snowstorm has just passed through. In that case, Arapahoe will have more powder to track up than Keystone, which is not only lower, but always more crowded.

A-Basin really comes into its own in springtime. The high-altitude sun bouncing off the reflector-oven walls of its high alpine bowls quickly transforms the snow here into the most consistent corn in Colorado. And when other areas are closing in early April, the scene at A-Basin is just warming up, literally and figuratively. All the good Colorado skiers I know treat themselves to an after-season ski season at Arapahoe. It's part of the normal ritual and tradition of skiing in this state. Of course, you have to change your strategy a bit. No one wants to ski icy moguls in the early morning (see the following *Ski Tech* section for more spring snow strategies). In spring there is an optimum time slot for almost every exposure.

You'll also want to eat at the outdoor barbecue at the warming hut on top of Exhibition lift. Or bring a picnic and find a flat dry rock somewhere under the *East Wall*. On an average-to-good snow year the lifts keep running until June. But as May wears on and even the snow at 12,000 feet starts to thin out, Arapahoe skiers often drive on up to Loveland Pass and with a little hiking along gentle ridge tops can usually find beautiful untracked corn-snow lines leading back down to the highway on either side of the pass. One of the most famous (or infamous) out-of-bounds runs at Arapahoe is a steep smooth face called "the Professor" that drops down across the road from the A-Basin parking lot. The Professor is completely outside and separate from the ski area; it's uncontrolled and can be (has been) a death-trap in winter. Don't take foolish risks for a few powder turns; far better to wait until late spring weather has solidified all the out-of-area slopes around Loveland pass before hiking out there for an adventure. If springtime corn snow up on the pass is still fairly solid in late morning, it's safe.

ARAPAHOE BASIN DATA

KEY PHONE NUMBERS See Keystone Data page.

TRANSPORTATION By car, 15 minutes up the canyon from Keystone
See Keystone Data.

MOUNTAIN STATISTICS

Vertical Drop	1,670 feet	Number of Lifts	5
Summit Elevation	12,450 feet	Uphill Capacity	6,200 skiers/hour
Base Elevation	10,780 feet	Longest Run	1 1/2 miles
Skiing Terrain	350 acres	Snowboarding	Yes

Keystone tickets are good at Arapahoe Basin

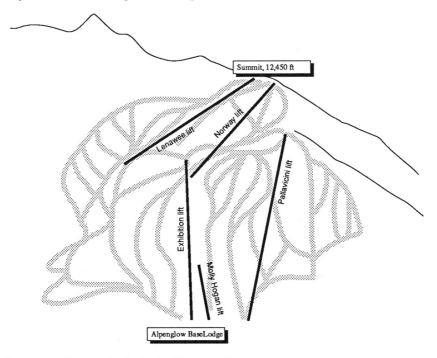

Sketch map of Arapahoe Basin showing lifts and main runs.
For greater detail and more specifics, consult current ski area trail maps.

Spring snow conditions can be both the best and the worst surfaces a skier ever gets to play on, or curse at – all on the same day. Variable, challenging, sublime. Spring snow is the result of repeated daily melting and nightly freezing. And during the day it goes through three distinct stages.

Early in the morning, spring snow is simply ice. Not the smooth polished ice that racers love to hone their carving skills on. Morning ice in spring is lumpy brutal stuff with every rut, every track, every glob of slush thrown up the previous evening turned into a rock-hard obstacle. Icy slopes on a spring morning have no redeeming qualities.

As the snow surface melts toward midday, it mellows into a condition that skiers call "corn." Corn snow is to skiers what sweet corn is to the inhabitants of Garrison Keeler's Lake Wobegone, a delight that banishes all the trials of their existence. This is the ultimate snow surface on which a good skier can do anything, accomplish miracles. Skis bite cleanly, hold effortlessly, slide smoothly, come alive.

Alas, perfect corn conditions only last from about 10:30 in the morning to 1:00 PM. Then, as the thawing/melting penetrates deeper into the snowpack, corn turns to slush, soupy glop that is challenging, annoying and occasionally dangerous to ski in. As usual, there are tricks to tame it.

Early in the morning you have two choices: Sleep in. Or head directly for east-facing slopes that have already been thawing in the sun for a couple of hours. Lumpy spring ice can't be tamed, shouldn't be skied. And in fact, the idea of watching the sun and choosing your slopes accordingly works all day long. If east-facing slopes are the first to "corn up," they are also the first to turn slushy in early afternoon. By then you should have moved around to the opposite, westerly exposures that are just starting to get good.

Unlike lumpy morning ice, afternoon slush can be skied well. The problem is the opposite of a smooth icy slope, where there isn't enough friction. Here there is too much. If you twist your skis violently, they won't skid. They'll simply catch or stick in the glue-like snow, knocking you off balance or worse. The remedy is simple, minimum twisting action, longer turns, allowing your skis to slice forward much more than they move sideways. Minimalist skiing.

On late spring afternoons, moguls can become dangerously soft. The danger, in fact, lies in burying the front of your skis in a soft bump. At that point only perfectly functioning bindings stand between you and an injury. To avoid coming this close, try to slide diagonally into slushy spring moguls so that your ski tips never hit the back side of the bump directly. Or better yet, quit early and go swimming. After three hours of sweet corn, why fight it?

CHAPTER 11   BRECKENRIDGE

Breckenridge is the princess of Summit County ski areas. Like its neighbors it offers a lot of skiing on an up-to-date modern mountain, but unlike Keystone and Copper, Breckenridge is a real town, a genuine Colorado ski town.

So many of Colorado's ski towns were mining towns, yet they're all different. Even today, with tee-shirt shops fast becoming the universal common denominator of the American resort landscape, their differing architecture tells a very different story. Aspen was a silver mining center, Crested Butte a proletarian coal mining community, Telluride a remote gold camp.... While Breckenridge was a famous placer mining district. Surreal gravel bars and placer gravel mounds greet you as you drive in from Lake Dillon, In winter these ghostly white lumps might be the leftover moguls from a vanished race of giant skiers. The Ten Mile range above echoes these same dome-like shapes in large white rolls that make skiers drool. No need to drool. Peaks 8 and 9 are spider-webbed with lifts, and now Peak 10 has just come on line.

Take your choice: an above-timberline bowl, gentle and forgiving trail cruising or some of the narrowest, gnarliest (a compliment in the bump skier's vocabulary) bump runs in the state. When I interviewed French World Cup Mogul Champ, Eric Berton, half our conversation revolved around the exceptionally challenging bumps of Breckenridge, a favorite annual stop on the World Cup bump circuit. But Breckenridge is a very balanced ski mountain: lots of terrain for the "rest of us," and some unusually inviting first-timer and beginner runs too. And there's the added plus of "downtown" Breckenridge, a multicolored Victorian main-street strip, running like the border stripe of a handwoven rug beneath mixed layers of condos and forest....

A BRECKENRIDGE OVERVIEW

Coincidentally the ten-mile range has ten major summits, logically although prosaically named Peaks 1 through 10, like a row of giant windswept milestones. The town of Breckenridge lies under the slopes of Peak 9, at one end of the range. And while the ski area doesn't reach all the way to the top of this imposing series of peaks, the rounded frontal ridges and the deep-cleft valleys between Peaks 8, 9 and 10 define the playing field at Breckenridge, divide the area into distinct zones, and directly shape your skiing day.

On the north end of the ski area, Peak 8 offers steeper skiing, open bowls, and a graceful mixture of sparse timberline trees with open slopes. For serious skiers.

The valley or gully between Peaks 8 and 9 is intense: steep, "rad," and thoroughly bumped out. On both sides of this drainage but especially on the so-called North Face of Peak 9, young bump specialists find the tightest, most challenging lines at Breckenridge.

Peak 9 is a mountain for the masses. Its front side is all hyper-friendly, non-challenging skiing. The lower half is strictly for beginners. The upper half of Peak 9 is low-key, low-intermediate skiing.

Moving over one more mountain, Peak 10, which was only recently opened by a new quad lift, completes the spectrum with what I'd call classic upper intermediate skiing: blue and black runs that aren't too demanding but still keep your attention.

Once you have this zone by zone overview of what can otherwise be a very spread-out and confusing ski mountain, it's duck soup to tailor your Breckenridge experience to your own level of skill, your own desire for challenge or calm. We'll look at each zone in more detail:

PEAK 9, A PERFECT WARM-UP MOUNTAIN

Peak 9 is the middle mountain, and actually offers pretty much middle-of-the-road, or middle-of-the-piste, skiing. It's also the mountain you reach if you take a lift directly up from town. The lower slopes are served by Colorado's (and we've been told, the world's) first quad super chair, and they are a pleasant maze of extremely gentle green beginners' runs. This is Breckenridge's main novice ski zone, and it's too flat for experienced skiers to do anything more than schuss on through. This is also where I would recommend that beginners take lessons at Breckenridge, even though there is a second ski school location at the base of Peak 8, which also has a small zone of easy green practice runs. There's much more easy terrain over here at the base of Peak 9, and what beginners need most, after a patient instructor, is lots

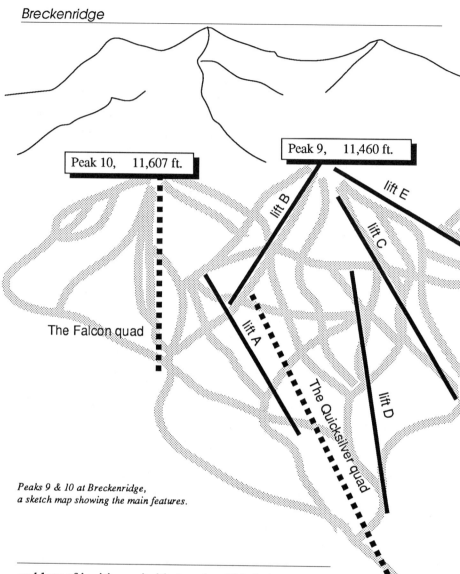

Peak 10, 11,607 ft.

Peak 9, 11,460 ft.

lift E

lift B

lift C

lift A

The Falcon quad

The Quicksilver quad

lift D

Peaks 9 & 10 at Breckenridge,
a sketch map showing the main features.

and lots of inviting suitable terrain. This is it.

The upper half of Peak 9 is laced with attractive,
meandering blue runs — the sort of intermediate skiing
that doesn't pose any special challenges or offer any special
rewards, just basic wandering trails, steep enough to slide along
at a good clip but never steep enough to make you want to put on
the brakes. For me these runs don't have much charm, but I recognize
that they are exactly what an enormous number of skiers need to develop
early parallel skills and confidence. Peak 9 is a great "learning mountain," and even for better skiers, it's a good place to warm up and get

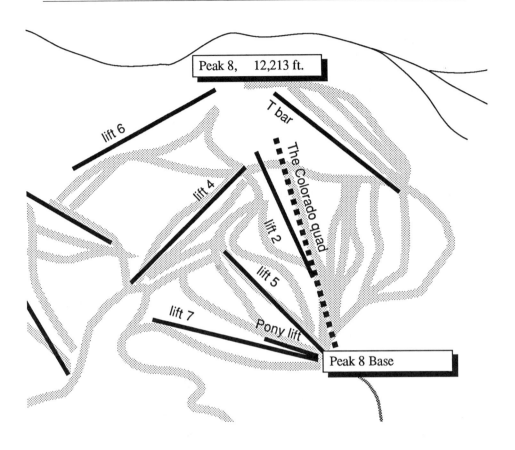

Peak 8 at Breckenridge, a sketch map showing the main runs and lifts.
For greater detail check the current ski area trail map
which is drawn to a larger scale and shows
the names and difficulty of all runs.

your ski legs back on the first day of a Summit County vacation.

PEAK 8, THE PEAK EXPERIENCE AT BRECKENRIDGE

Peak 8 has a good deal more character. It lies north of Peak 9 (to the right looking up from town) and is set back from and above the village. Its higher altitude partly explains its more alpine feeling. You reach Peak 8 by a winding five-minute drive up Ski Hill Road from town, or by skiing across from Peak 9, which can be daunting for non-bumpers, unless they follow an easy green catwalk called *Union*.

Stronger skiers in search of excitement and intriguing terrain will spend most of their Breckenridge ski time on Peak 8. The lower half of this mountain is striped with steeper blue and moderate black runs, whose most characteristic features are big swooping rolls and dips (very different from the more uniform pitch of Peak 9 runs). Although these are all trails cut through thick forest, they don't seem as closed-in as many forested trails do.

But the magic lives on the upper slopes of Peak 8, where the ski area emerges into wide-open, treeless terrain. *Contest Bowl* and *Horseshoe Bowl* are the centerpieces: smooth steep white basins that remind me a lot of the high open bowls at Mammoth Mountain in the Sierra. Their peculiar wind exposure also produces a wonderful snow condition that I tend to associate with Mammoth — wind-packed powder: cold and smooth, hard but grippy, ideal for snappy rebounding turns.

It takes a little gumption to get the most out of Peak 8. *Horseshoe Bowl* is served by a T-bar, and you have to walk some from its top to reach the best lines. Worth every step. To the right of this T-Bar, you'll find a zone of indistinct black and blue lines among patchy high-altitude trees that are probably the least known, least skied runs at Breckenridge. *Forget-Me-Not* and *White Crown* feel almost out of bounds, which they almost are.

In fact, adventurous skiers looking up from town or from the slopes of Peak 8 at the softly curving white bowls receding back toward higher, farther ridges will wonder aloud: "Why didn't they put the ski area up *there*? Why aren't there lifts to takes us back *there*?" This is the same sort of question that any European skier would ask on seeing Colorado ski areas for the first time: "Why did they put the ski area down among the trees instead of up there in all that white emptiness?" At Breck-enridge, some of this white expanse is available – and you'll love it – but there's a lot more beyond the ski area boundary markers. High-altitude untracked powder has tempted local skiers for a long time. But skiers who go beyond boundaries in Colorado need a lot of judgment and at least a little luck. Avalanches, at Breckenridge and elsewhere, have claimed skiers that didn't have enough of one or the other. Personally I'm hoping that areas like Breckenridge will progressively open up more and more of this "beyond the ropes" terrain to their skiing guests, controlling and stabilizing the snow, and providing lift access to these wide open spaces.

One of the main reasons that areas haven't wanted to build lifts up into the high country above timberline is the uncertainty of the snow conditions. Some years the wind can scour the high ridges and basins bare, while other seasons this high terrain is a powder paradise. So it doesn't make sense to build expensive and exposed chairlifts above timberline. Fortunately surface lifts are making a comeback. Recently installed platter-pull lifts at Copper Mountain, Crested Butte and Vail open up splendid treeless terrain. And no one complains about the Horseshoe Bowl T-bar at Breckenridge. In the long run, opening up high basins with surface lifts is more cost effective than cutting new runs in dense forest; and it provides a perfect counterpoint to the sort of skiing usually served by modern high-speed quads. A complementary side of the white revolution. I want more!

Half into and half out of this white world above timberline are the runs known as the "back bowls" of Peak 8. These are more designated lines than cut runs, fanning out and down from chair 6, the Snowbird lift. This is an ideal area for creative skiing: threading new paths through partly timbered, partly open, reasonably steep but never scary terrain. An area to explore as well as ski.

BUMPETY, BUMPETY, BUMP

Bump skiers tend to hang out on the steep sides of the valley or gulch that separates Peak 8 from Peak 9, where you'll find the most demanding technical skiing at Breckenridge. I know most Colorado skiers, and most of the readers of this guide, are not wild about bump skiing. But I think this zone is worth a special mention because of the importance of freestyle and mogul competition in the Breckenridge story.

Breckenridge began to host international freestyle competitions – moguls, ballet and aerials – years ago, fostering the development of this exciting, gymnastic branch of ski competition in a period when it was generally misunderstood and ignored. In this, Breckenridge was ahead of its time since mogul skiing has only recently been recognized as a full gold-medal Olympic event, just in time for the winter games in France. World Cup freestyle events are still an annual event at Breckenridge, the only international freestyle competitions in Colorado. Naturally, with this freestyle bias, Breckenridge was one of the first mountains in Colorado to encourage snowboarding. Bravo! My hat's off.

The difficult bump runs I mentioned are concentrated in two pods on either side of the gulch between Peaks 8 and 9. The runs on the north face of Peak 9 are the wildest, meanest and the most fun when you survive them. Runs like *Mine Shaft* and *Devil's Crotch* are extremely narrow, sometimes only two or three moguls wide, and absolutely unrelenting. No flats, no rest spots. You just get in the groove and go. By comparison, the four double black diamond runs on the opposite

southern side of the gulch, from *Southern Cross* to *Mach 1*, seem
positively forgiving. They are almost as steep and every bit as moguled,
but there's so much more room to maneuver that you are almost over-
whelmed with choices. A serious workout for strong skiers.

PEAK 10, NEW KID ON THE BLOCK

Peak 10 is the newest addition at Breckenridge, opened up in one
fell swoop by one new lift, a super quad naturally. You reach Peak 10
by skiing across from the upper slopes of Peak 9; or, from town, take the
Quicksilver quad and cut sharp left at the top. This is not nearly as big
an area as the other two "peaks," but it's a perfect complement to exist-
ing skiing here. Peak 10 saves the southern end of Breckenridge from
the dreaded epithet, "boring," because it adds precisely what the central
slopes lack: stimulating upper intermediate skiing and even some
seriously advanced pitches. On the left of the lift, looking up, you'll
find the most popular Peak 10 skiing – easy blacks and solid blues. Although I find these runs, like so many recently cut trails in the West, a
little too narrow. I don't know whether it's a case of ecological consciousness vis à vis tree cutting, timidity, or laziness, but ski areas today
don't seem to be cutting runs as wide as they used to, and it's a real
shame.

The surprise treats on Peak 10 are the harder runs to the north of the
lift (on the right side as you ride up). *Spitfire* and *Corsair* are narrow
steep and serious. But best of all is *The Burn*, a mountain flank where
lightning and a forest fire did the sort of radical clearing that ski areas
can't. For years, skiers coasting down *Upper Lehman*, the gully run
dividing Peaks 9 and 10 have looked up and thought of this steep open
burn. Sometimes they would hike and traverse up into it to enjoy one
perfect set of tracks. Now it's lift-served. In lighter snow years these
steep runs on Peak 10 may not be open, but they still give a lot of
character and drama to this end of the mountain.

BRECKENRIDGE, TOWNSCAPES AND TOWN TIPS

Breckenridge is an honest no-nonsense ski town with just enough
history on Main Street to let you know it's been here for a long time,
enough modern lodging blocks stacked up the hill behind Main Street to
pamper an enormous number of skiers, enough garishly painted false
fronts to suggest that someone is trying to turn this town into a cutesy
little theme park for skiers, and enough locals who still care to make you
hope it won't happen. One friend of mine calls Breckenridge a "middle-
class Aspen." But I don't think that quite captures it, even though

Breckenridge prices aren't nearly as alarming as Aspen's, or Vail's. And one has to take a mountain town seriously when it boasts two bookstores.

You won't exactly need a map to orient yourself in Breckenridge, as Main Street is where everything is, where everything happens. It's a real walking street: human in scale, full of goodies, and a scene that will certainly take you more than one evening to explore.

My village favorites include: The Terrace, the finest restaurant in town; and for variety and a different sort of atmosphere altogether, The Briar Rose, which has to qualify as Breckenridge's traditional or classic good restaurant. Breakfasts and Mexican food at the Gold Pan. And when you tire of run-of-the-mill ski-town shopping, visit the Hibberd McGrath Gallery at the corner of Main Street and Ski Hill Road. Here you'll find work by some of the country's top artisan-craftspeople – and shows that would not be out of place in New York or San Francisco.

BRECKENRIDGE DATA

KEY PHONE NUMBERS

Snow Conditions	(303) 453-6118
Ski Area Information	(303)453-2368
Central Reservations	(303) 453-2918

TRANSPORTATION

By car, 90 minute drive (in good road and weather conditions) from Denver on I-70 west to Breckenridge exit (#203), then south on Colorado Highway 9.

By bus or van, from Denver's Stapleton Airport. Rental cars also available at the airport. Daily Continental Trailways bus from Denver and Grand Junction.

MOUNTAIN STATISTICS

Vertical Drop	2,613 feet
Summit Elev.	12,213 feet
Base Elevation	9,600 feet
Skiing Terrain	1,880 acres
Number of Lifts	15 including 2 high-speed detachable quad chairs and 1 surface lift
Uphill Capacity	22,650 skiers per hour
Longest run	3 miles
Snowboarding	Yes

Four and six day Ski the Summit passes are available, good at Breckenridge, Copper and Keystone.

SKI TECH: A SNOWBOARDING PRIMER

Few things are as humbling or as stimulating to a good skier as abandoning the security of a sport already mastered to become, once again, an awkward beginner. This is true on cross-country skating skis, on telemark skis, on monoskis, and especially on snowboards. Last winter I strapped on one of these amazing contraptions for the first time and loved it. Here's a little of what I learned:

Which foot forward? Snowboarding like surfing and skateboarding is a sideways-standing sport. To discover your natural stance find an icy stretch of pavement or a frozen puddle, run a few feet and let yourself slide across it. Which foot do you instinctively stretch forward? That's your front foot on a snowboard.

Getting started. Pick an easy hill with soft snow. And what precisely does one do with a snowboard? Go across the hill. You will gain more confidence and control, more quickly, if you develop a traversing/sideslipping/braking pattern first, before heading down the fall line. Unlike skiing, traversing across a slope on a snowboard is quite different depending on which way you're heading. You will have a backside traverse (back to the mountain) and a front side traverse (facing the mountain). The backside traverse is a stronger, easier maneuver because the high plastic spoilers of snowboard bindings give you more support in this direction – you can lean back against them to increase edging. On the frontside traverse you feel like you're standing on your toes, and it takes more strength to control the board.

Flatten and sideslip your board as you traverse the slope; and to stop, push the board away from you, twisting it up the hill, while you let it sideslip. Oh – very important – when you get in trouble, sit down! In fact, you can sit down and flip your board around between traverse until you're ready to turn downhill. As in skiing, the downhill turn is the soul of the sport, but don't try it till you feel comfortable just sliding sideways and across the hill. When you're ready, start the turn by committing your body in the direction you want to go — lead with your front hand – and then swivel the board with your feet to catch up to where your body already is. The feeling is almost like falling into a turn, insecure but effective.

This thumbnail sketch doesn't take the place of lessons, and since more and more ski schools are hiring snowboarding specialists, it won't be hard to find such lessons at progressive ski areas. A few years ago it would have been impossible. Good sliding!

CHAPTER 12   COPPER MOUNTAIN

I've had some great days skiing at Copper Mountain, and although there's no doubt it deserves a spot in a guidebook devoted to the best skiing in Colorado, I still have mixed feelings about this last Summit County resort. Copper Mountain is an under-achiever. It's good but could be, and should be better. What I like best at Copper is the natural logic of its mountain, what I like least is the characterless and chaotic "village" development at its base, a missed opportunity if ever there was one. What I just don't know is whether it's too late for Copper Mountain to grow into the sort of attractive, integrated, human-scale resort village that should have been planned and built from the beginning....

Imagine a mountain, a grand mountain, whose main axis seems to be horizontal rather than vertical, stretching sideways around the fork of an alpine valley rather than up toward the sky and you get a sense of Copper's paradoxical topography. Sounds weird, skis great. Copper must have been designed by the great forest ranger in the sky just to keep different levels of skiers from getting in each other's hair. Looking up from the base you see a beginners' mountain on the far right, a steep bumped-out experts' mountain on the far left, and the smoothest gradation of ski terrain imaginable in between. From wherever you find yourself, you can move one run to the east and the skiing will be a fraction harder, one run further west and the slope will be a tad gentler and easier. I don't know any other mountain where average skiers can fine-tune the degree of challenge they'll face on each run quite this easily.

PLUSES AND MINUSES ON THE MOUNTAIN

Since I've decided to be honestly critical of certain aspects of the Copper Mountain experience, the least I can do is offset my criticism with some well deserved praise. Copper Mountain was one of the first Colorado areas in recent years to make a serious effort to open up some of that tantalizing treeless skiing that's always been waiting just out of reach, above timberline. And it's been a grand success.

They've done it in a logical, step by step way: first with a surface lift to open up *Spaulding* and *Hallelujah Bowls* directly above what used to be the highest point on the ski mountain. And then last year with lift S, off to the right, opening some serious, even magical skiing in *Union Bowl* and on the slopes of *Union Peak*.

The conventional wisdom in Colorado used to be that skiers would find such slopes too exposed to sun and wind, too difficult to enjoy, that only tree-sheltered powder was really any good, that lifts would be hard to run up there above timberline, in short that it wouldn't work. Copper has proved otherwise in the last few years. And I think other ski areas too are starting to get the message. Copper today is a far more exciting mountain to ski on than it was five years ago.

At the same time, here at Copper, we see the reverse side of the coin. They have done something else that tends to take the excitement right out of skiing, something I find incomprehensible. Almost every mountain has a few designated slow-skiing zones: usually and quite justifiably at crowded trail intersections near the bottom of popular lifts. But Copper has gone too far. They use a yellow diamond-shaped caution symbol and yellow shading to designate slow-skiing zones on their trail map. And when you look twice, slow-skiing symbols are almost all you can see. Yellow everywhere. It's absurd; even steep black runs have gotten the slow-skiing treatment. And last season, the Copper Mountain ski patrol seemed determined to enforce this slow-skiing policy with a strictness that made California highway patrolmen look lighthearted by comparison. Almost all the blue intermediate runs in the center of the mountain have been transformed into speed traps. This is not the way to run a user-friendly ski area. The fact is that other Colorado areas don't have such oppressive slow-skiing policies and that Copper is no safer for it – and a lot less enjoyable. The silliest thing about it is that, because of Copper's unique left-to-right difficulty spectrum (the mountain steepening as you move east and flattening as you move west), this area has fewer problems than most with skiers of different levels getting in each other's way. In future editions of this guide I hope to be able to write that this strange policy is no longer in force....

And finally, not to end this section on a sour note , Copper deserves kudos for its early season slope preparation. They have a lot of snowmaking and use it well, generally opening a limited number of runs with very good cover long before Thanksgiving. The US ski team has traditionally used Copper Mountain for early season training; and a lot

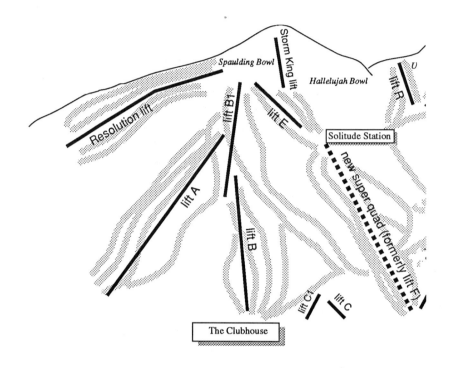

The eastern or steeper side of Copper Mountain, a sketch map showing the lifts and main runs. For a more accurate and detailed view, consult a current ski area trail map.

of my friends, ski instructors and ski fanatics, do too. There's no doubt that Copper, along with Keystone, offers the best early, early season skiing in Colorado.

COPPER FOR LESS EXPERIENCED SKIERS

There are several "base" clusters at Copper. The Clubhouse (next to lift B) at the far left side is for strong skiers only. The Center is indeed right there, in the center of the mountain, and from here lift F slants up and slightly left toward intermediate and advanced skiing, while lift G and the new American Flyer quad slant up and right toward more modest lower-intermediate and beginner skiing. The final base pod, Union Creek, is still further right, and its lifts serve really easy terrain. True novice skiers should start here, from Union Creek.

Such novice skiers get short changed at a lot of Colorado ski areas

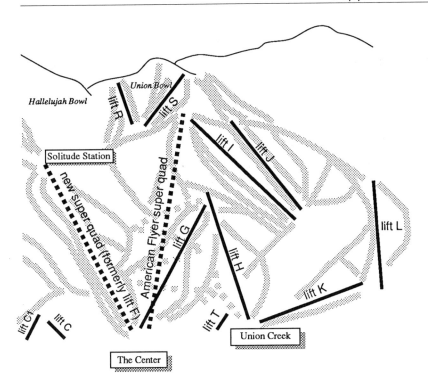

The western or gentler side of Copper Mountain.
Note that the center section of the mountain overlaps on these two pages.

where you have to be a pretty fair intermediated to ski and enjoy the whole mountain, or "ski it from the top." At Copper, very weak or inexperienced skiers can still have a major mountain adventure by riding the American Flyer quad and then circling around to the extreme far right or western side of the area on a gentle green called *Soliloquy.* You can continue this far-west circle tour by skiing *Roundabout* or *West Ten Mile* over by lift L, a very quiet gentle backwater on the mountain. This makes an enormously long run, but the final return to Union Creek is almost painfully flat with nature taking care of the slow-skiing injunction. For a better finish, cut right on *Soliloquy* where *Roundabout* branches off and follow *Woodwinds* to the bottom.

   Another "mountain adventure" on all-green slopes – but somewhat more demanding – is to ski down from the top of lift R into *Copper Tone* and then follow *Care Free* to the bottom. The two top choices, *Union*

Park or Wheeler Creek, are unusually attractive greens and have a
totally different, upper-mountain feel than all the other easy skiing on
the western side of Copper Mountain. Less skilled skiers are beautifully
served at Copper.

COPPER FOR STRONG SKIERS

Very strong skiers will find happiness clear across the mountain, on
lifts A and B which rise from the valley floor, and Resolution lift higher
up, as well as on the two above-timberline zones I've mentioned. The
only consistent disappointment is *Enchanted Forest*, a mouthwatering
area of half-open bowls and thin sparse trees descending from the
shoulder of *Hallelujah Bowl* toward the middle mountain drainage of
Wheeler Creek and *Copper Tone. Enchanted Forest* has almost never
been open when I've visited Copper Mountain and seems to be especially prone to wind, which scours its ridge-like upper slopes into veri-
table rock gardens.

The runs on chairs A and B are straight medium-steep bump slopes.
Chair A gets less traffic, and so its bumps often seem better shaped. But
the best skiing of all for strong skiers is found in the high bowls above
timberline that I talked about earlier. This is the real thing. A nice
linkup is to ski *Spaulding Bowl* from the top of the Storm King poma
and then continue on down *Highline*, my favorite among the four black
runs served by the Resolution lift. It's obvious that the exciting new
runs on Union Peak are an exception to my sweeping generalization
about the skiing getting easier and easier as you move west on this
mountain. That's okay, all generalizations have exceptions and the east-
west spectrum of difficulty is still a good overview of how Copper
Mountain works.

The only class of skiers who may feel a little left out on this mountain is the gung-ho, go-for-it intermediate, the skier who skis hard but
not really well enough to handle black slopes with ease. There just
aren't many attractive blue runs in the center of the mountain that
haven't been designated slow-skiing zones. Hopefully this will change
in time; and certainly the recent upgrading of Lift F (from The Center to
Solitude Station) to full detachable quad status will improve the experience in the very center of this wide mountain. At the very least, it will
speed up the access to *Spaulding* and *Hallelujah Bowls* for strong skiers,
as well as helping skiers move across the mountain faster. There are
also some good intermediate cruisers over on lifts I and J, (the other exception to my east-west rule), but it's a long way to go for a couple of
cut-loose runs.

RESORT DESIGN REVISITED, PROS AND CONS

Copper is an attractive looking resort. There's a lot of nice architecture spread out along the base of the mountain on the narrow flat valley floor beside the I-70 freeway. And I particularly like the amount of actual copper that's been used, both as roofs and architectural trim. As appropriate as it is good looking. But the rub is that all this good architecture has been lavished on semi-detached condominium blocks, not on an attractive pedestrian center that can draw skiers in and provide a real focus for after ski living in the base village. Truth is, it's not a village at all, but merely a resort "development" in which cars and parking lots got as much or more attention in the planning process as people.

The closest thing to a real village center at Copper Mountain is the Mountain Plaza, a handsome elevated square with a cluster of shops and eateries, set amid some really good-looking highrise lodging. Trouble is, there just isn't enough of it for the Mountain Plaza to become a social center of gravity for the resort. But it's also true that a lot of skiers prefer to sample a broad cross-section of Summit County skiing in the course of a week: skiing a couple of days at Copper, a couple at Keystone and Breckenridge for a really diverse ski experience. An option made easier by the availability of a three-mountain week-long pass. For such skiers, the lack of a strong village atmosphere at Copper Mountain isn't such a minus.

But if you do want to ski Copper for a week and you're looking for the sort of social grace and resort atmosphere that's in short supply here, you can't do better than spending that week with the Club Med. The Club Med ski formula is simple, they create a village within the village with a non-stop social life of its own. A few years ago I taught skiing at a Club Med "village" in the Alps, and I can tell you that it's a formula that really works. It works particularly well at Copper Mountain, where it supplies the sort of lively animation that this resort lacks.

COPPER MOUNTAIN DATA

KEY PHONE NUMBERS

Snow Conditions

(303) 968-2100
(303) 893-1400 (Denver)

Ski Area Information

(303) 968-2882

Central Reservations

800 458-8386

TRANSPORTATION

By car, one hour and 45 minutes drive (in good road and weather
conditions) from Denver on I-70
to Copper Mountain exit (#195).
By bus or limo, from Denver's Stapleton Airport.

MOUNTAIN STATISTICS

Vertical Drop   2,760 feet
Summit Elev.   12,360 feet
Base Elevation   9,600 feet
Skiing Terrain   1,180 acres
Longest Run   2.8 miles
Number of Lifts   20 including 2 high-speed detachable quad chair
                   and 4 surface lifts
Uphill Capacity   28,250 skiers per hour
Snowboarding   Yes

Four and six day Ski the Summit passes are available, good at
Breckenridge, Copper and Keystone.

Copper Mountain has been associated with the US Ski Team and with the Alpine National Championships for so many years that I thought it would be appropriate to talk about ski racing in this Ski Tech section. For most skiers, racing is synonymous with NASTAR, the national standard race held at hundreds of ski areas across the country: an open, single-flag, giant-slalom type race where skiers compete against a base time established by a designated pacesetter. Almost every skier has run a NASTAR race or two, but very few have achieved their full potential between the gates. Here are two simple tips to improve your NASTAR handicap.

Turn early. This is the key advice, and it's so simple I'm always amazed more skiers haven't figured it out. Don't wait until you reach the flag that you have to turn around before starting that turn. If you start your turn at the flag itself, you will invariably turn too hard (to aim back at the next flag) and in so doing you will find yourself skidding down below the optimum fastest line between the two flags. Instead start your turn well before you reach the flag, curving around in a wider, longer arc, so that when you actually pass the flag, your turn is complete and you are already aimed for the next flag! This way you will be making a rounder longer turn, but you won't skid down below the optimum line – which is where most skiers lose time.

Step your turns. This one is simple too. Instead of turning both skis, step dynamically to the side on the ski which is going to become the outside ski of the turn, and make your turn completely on that ski. Why? By stepping to the side you can gain a foot or more of extra distance away from the pole, which gives you more room to complete your turn early, without waiting to get by the pole before making your move. The final result: a smoother run, no sudden jerky turns, no skidding low in your turns, and a better NASTAR handicap. Five, four, three, two, one, go!

PART V   THE SOULFUL SOUTHWEST

CHAPTER 13   CRESTED BUTTE

Crested Butte is both an exciting if medium-sized ski resort and a magical small town – a "beaut" any way you spell it – nestled on the southern side of the Elk range, just an overnight ski tour away from Aspen, but seemingly a world away. Indeed it is another world. Driving from Aspen to Crested Butte, one would have to circumnavigate three sides of a massive mountain range, an epic drive. And when you got there....

Like all of Colorado's most romantic ski towns, Crested Butte was originally a mining settlement. But here men mined coal not gold, and there's an earthiness, a funky down-home simplicity about the Butte today that must have its roots in this particular past. As a coal-mining town Crested Butte couldn't put on airs, as a ski town it doesn't chose to. Charm yes, glitz no.

How can I introduce you in a few words to Crested Butte's very special character? There's the countryside: a broad open ranching valley that reminds me of long, lonesome Wyoming ranch country. There's the old town of Crested Butte, a few miles away from the base of the ski mountain. Here you find one of the most vital small towns in the Rockies; a town that pulled together to defeat a giant molybdenum corporation's big-buck plans to turn the southern Elk mountains into a slag heap; a town living its own life behind old-time wooden false fronts, sharing its Main Street with winter tourists instead of simply turning it over to them. And there's the new town of Mt. Crested Butte, up at the base of the ski area. Mt. Crested Butte is fundamentally a tourist lodging community whose modern condos and lodges are in no small measure responsible for preserving the charm of old Crested Butte from ski-development pressures that would have altered it irrevocably, and not for the better. And there's the mountain itself, a curiously shaped plug of a peak, really and truly named Crested Butte; and the ski mountain grafted onto it, generally a rather good if not ultra-modern ski area, with at least two amazing advantages. First, Crested Butte is blessed with the best weather pattern in the state, lying at the overlapping intersection of southerly and northerly storm tracks – snow city. And second, an experts' mountain, the *North Face*, right beside the regular ski mountain that in my opinion offers the finest "adventure skiing" in Colorado. Have I whet you appetite? Let's look closer.

THE WAY THE MOUNTAIN WORKS

Unlike so many ski mountains, Crested Butte doesn't exactly have a front side or a back. It has a front, a side valley, an upper "around-the corner" side, which is the *North Face* area I'm so crazy about, a lower "around-the-corner" area called *East River*, and just to confuse matters, a small subsidiary area of easy skiing, quite detached from the rest of the mountain across a sort of low pass. Complex, but I want to give you at least a general impression of the rich topography of this area.

The new town of Mt Crested Butte sits in a sunny almost treeless saddle underneath the Butte itself. And, as is the case with Steamboat, the wide white treeless lower slopes coming into town remind me a lot of the Alps. Crested Butte itself is a very distinctive looking peak, a sharp pointed, art-director's idea of a mountain. But the summit that you can admire from the valley is more rock than snow, so the ski area is located just beside it – with the peak and its rocky ribs looming off on your right as you ride one of several lifts out of the village of Mt.Crested Butte. On the right, the Silver Queen chair takes you up as close as you can get to the pointed peak and opens up a steep front face full of classic black runs. A second chair, the Keystone lift, slants up and left, crossing and serving a much gentler area of the front face with a host of meandering green runs. But from the top of both of these lifts you can drop over a sort of ridge into *Paradise*, a parallel valley running sideways and down to the left, which is the heart of the intermediate or "blue" skiing on this mountain.

"Paradise" is also the name of one of the two chairs that serves this lovely intermediate basin, and is formally attached to *Paradise Bowl*, a large open area up at the head of this drainage, the first area on your right as you ski down from Paradise lift. But you can call the whole shooting match back here *Paradise*, and everyone will know what you're taking about. Runs here are all honest blue, longish, with some flatter sections near the bottom, and very pleasant indeed. The Paradise chair serves every run back here, and is longer with a lot more vertical than the parallel Teocalli chair. The only reason for riding the Teocalli

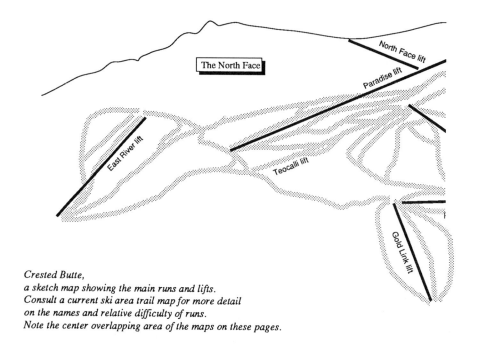

Crested Butte,
a sketch map showing the main runs and lifts.
Consult a current ski area trail map for more detail
on the names and relative difficulty of runs.
Note the center overlapping area of the maps on these pages.

lift is to get back to the point on the front ridge from where all the easy ways down the front fan out.

Continuing on below the bottom of Paradise or Teocalli lifts and trending rightward, around the corner, you come to a sort of separate one-lift ski area, *East River*. The chair here serves runs that are a little steeper and more continuous than those in Paradise. The black *East-River* runs are very friendly indeed. *Resurrection* is the best of them, a tilted boulevard of steep rolling steps. These runs dead end, of course, near the bottom of a wide river valley. And on the opposite, south-facing slopes, long treeless ridges will make you drool as you stand in line, waiting to come back up. The slopes on this "next-door" mountain have been pretty much stashed away behind a wilderness designation, so all skiers can do is daydream, or break out their touring skis.

But to me the most interesting part of Crested Butte is the long and rugged mountain face that rises in bold, cliff-like steps above *Paradise*, and looms high above *East River* – the *North Face*. This is experts-only country of a sort found at no other Colorado ski resort. The ski company

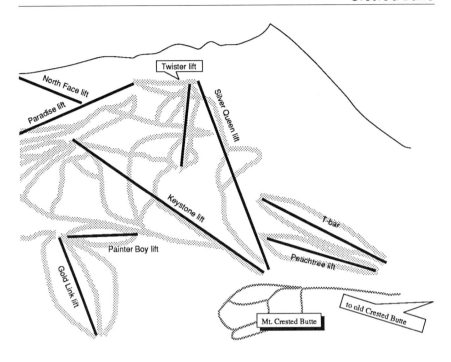

here deserves a lot of credit for opening this terrain up on a regular basis to the skiing public. And they did it in a brilliant, cost-effective way. A short two-minute poma ride from *Paradise Bowl* now replaces the strenuous half-hour climb which used to be skiers' only option to reach the *North Face*. This ridiculously small and inexpensive lift added 260 acres of the most dramatic, serious, ungroomed double-black-diamond skiing imaginable to the ski area; and in my book raised it into a whole different league! All it took was vision and commitment – two commodities not always in abundant supply in a ski industry progressively terrorized by the threat of lawsuits from skiers who want to be protected from their own lack of judgment at all costs.

Crested Butte's lifts, I might add, are otherwise not too distinguished. Except for this one imaginative platter-pull lift, the white revolution in ski lifts is only a distant rumor at this southwestern Colorado hideaway. There are no high-speed detachables yet, which is hardly a crisis because Crested Butte never draws the overflow weekend crowds that made super lifts a necessity at areas closer to Denver.

Did I mention the snow? Crested Butte lies at the snowy crossroads of Colorado's two winter weather patterns. It gets southerly storms that sweep up across Arizona, over Taos and Telluride; and it also get northern dumps roaring down from Canada that hit resorts like Steamboat and Winter Park. I've always encountered remarkable snow conditions here.

CRESTED BUTTE FOR LESS EXPERIENCED SKIERS

If my enthusiasm for the *North Face* has got your worried, relax. Learners, inexperienced skiers, and cautious conservative intermediates can have a great time at the Butte. Down in Mt. Crested Butte, off to the right, is a small practice lift, called Peachtree, with wide green slopes, totally out of the mountain's traffic pattern. I've already mentioned that all the runs underneath Keystone Lift are friendly, low angle greens. And I want to tell you about a zone that bolder skiers never seem to find at Crested Butte, but which is tailor made for cautious and inexperienced skiers. I think of it as the "North Pass" area, which is comprised of two lifts that stick off like a thumb in the opposite direction to everything else on the mountain. Painter Boy and Gold Link lifts are short chairs that serve flatish open sparsely timbered slopes on both sides of a low round side peak to the north of the Keystone runs. *Little Lizzie*, *Splain's Gulch* and *Topsy*, the gentle green runs that come down the Painter-Boy side are the only runs at Crested Butte that take one right through aspen woods, always a very esthetic experience. This is a lovely area to build mileage and confidence. Inexperienced skiers that want to test themselves in Paradise should first ski *Bushwhacker* down to the Teocalli lift, and only if that seems easy, then take the Paradise lift into upper *Paradise Bowl* which is considerably steeper.

FOR STRONG AND ADVENTUROUS SKIERS

Good skiers spend most of their time in the large *Paradise* area and on the *East River* runs – which, as the name hints, receive wonderful morning sunlight – but very good skiers in search of adventure will tend to ski these two zones only for a warm-up, and for a little R & R after particularly harrowing runs on the *North Face*. I'd also recommend that all classes of strong skiers, skiers who are skiing the whole mountain, eat lunch at one of the two mountain restaurants. It's a roundabout jaunt back to down to town, and you don't have a super quad to shoot you back up in a hurry.

Aside from the *North Face*, which we'll cover in a minute, there is one other zone of challenging expert skiing skiing near the top of the front face, served by the Twister chair. It's all relative though. These demanding, well banked runs are perfect racing trails, used for the Downhill and Super G at the US national championships. But they are simply steep trails, with nice fallaways, a sustained pitch, sweeping turns and sweeping views back over the valley toward old Crested Butte – Nice but nothing to get excited about. Further west (to the right as you ride up the Twister or Silver Queen lifts) are some more unusual sections of the mountain marked with telltale double black diamonds, a sure sign of excitement at the Butte. I use the term "sections" advisedly, because these are not cut runs but rather zones to explore. Yet *Peel* and *Upper Peel* are seldom in good shape, and often closed by the patrol, because wind sweeping around the peak tends to scour out the snow cover. When they're good they're worth hiking over to and checking out. But the *North Face* is generally a safer bet, and a much bigger playing field for ski adventure.

What do I mean by adventure skiing? Naturally I'm talking about skiing in an ungroomed and wild mountain setting, but I also mean skiing that demands judgment and imagination as well as technique. Skiing that's not obvious. That challenges you to think clearly as well as to move well. The *North Face* fits this description perfectly: if you ski in here carelessly, foolishly, you'll go right over a cliff, and it's bye bye baby, bye bye. No, it's certainly not a death trap, but it is very serious, and you could easily get into trouble back here. You can also easily have the time of your life back here too.

A good way of seeing whether you're up to it, is to ski the *Tower 11 Chutes* first. Instead of taking the *North Face* lift, just follow the right side of *Paradise Bowl* until you reach a marked gate in the boundary rope and traverse right to the chutes. These are openings in steep forest right under the Paradise lift line, and if you feel at home here, then the *North Face* will be your cup of tea. The logical strategy is to explore the *North Face* by skiing further across it each run. The first lines lead through what's called *The Glades*, next you'll traverse across to *High Life*, following a packed out hiking trail that everybody else up there follows, and then drop down into the *North Face* proper. Finally you'll want to see how far across this vast mountain face you can get, and you'll ski *Spellbound Bowl* and finally *Phoenix Bowl*.

What's it like? Don't be misled by the names. These aren't classic bowls, but rather open faces and wide steep gullies in a rugged step-like face that alternates almost at random between thick timber, cliffs and couloirs, and sudden, unexpected and always welcome mini-bowls and chutes of snow. A good line on the *North Face* may take you into and through several of these steep "bowls" or clearings in succession. The steep slot-like faces at the very bottom like *Cesspool*, *Last Steep*, *Staircase* and *Phoenix Steps* are the steepest of all, and a real challenge to ski well just when you are getting tired. There is usually a best, or most obvious line down any of these openings, and there are numerous variants. On some of these variants a fall is not a viable option. Finally, to really have a wonderful time back here, hook up with some local skiers. Exploring the *North Face* with Crested Butte friends doubling as guides, I've skied lines that I could never have found for myself, at least not easily. This is high energy skiing. Yahoooooooooooooo....

TELEMARKING AT THE BUTTE

There's another sort of ski adventure, forever associated with Crested Butte: telemarking. The Butte was the birthplace, and today remains a hotbed of the "telemark revolution"– that hard-to-explain, hard-to-resist mania for skiing even the toughest downhill runs on skinny skis with free-heel, cross-country bindings. You'll probably see more young telemark heroes at Crested Butte than anywhere else in Colorado. The Telemark turn is a rediscovered artifact from the dark ages of skiing and Nordic history, done in a semi-kneeling position, one foot and ski advanced, the other trailing. A singularly graceful and very athletic variant of skiing, definitely not for everyone. In fact, its main attraction, at least at ski areas, is its difficulty; and its main converts are gifted young alpine skiers, who have literally run out of challenges and are looking for something new, something harder. Well, let me be a little more precise – telemarking per se is not so hard, it is in fact an easy way to maneuver skinny cross-country skis in soft back-country snow. But telemarking down steep runs at a ski area is very hard indeed. If you're tempted, or just want to know more, read the next *Ski Tech* section. And consider taking an introductory telemark lesson while you're at Crested Butte.

ATMOSPHERE, APRES, VICTUALS AND LODGING

If you've gotten the idea that I like Crested Butte, you're right. This place is a gem of a ski resort. And although hardly unknown, the Butte has nowhere near the reputation of the big guys across the range, so one has a certain feeling of discovery skiing here for the first time. I enjoy the town as much as the mountain. The old town of Crested Butte, that is. While the new town of Mt. Crested Butte plays a vital skier service role – this is where most of the guest accommodations are located, and it's hard to beat the slopeside convenience – it's not a place I can get attached to. The hot apres-ski rendezvous up at the mountain is a big-room bistro called The Artichoke, which finally moved into its new location, filling up an empty foundation hole that had gapped like a missing tooth among the mountain village structures for the past few years. Mt. Crested, I must admit, has a very unfinished feel to it. With a little vision and a lot of money, this slopeside complex could still be saved from the messy future it's heading toward—a sprawl of disorganized condos and parking lots. There's still enough unbuilt space up there that one can close one's eyes and imagine a large underground parking lot with a handsome pedestrian village center above it. In the meantime, you can find every sort of lodging up there, including a full-on, full-service hotel, The Grand Butte. But when you feel like a night on the town, you'll inevitably take the shuttle bus to "town,"or drive your own car the few miles down the hill into old Crested Butte.

Life in town pulses up and down the main street, Elk Avenue, which is the narrowest main street of any Colorado mining town I know, something that gives it an especially intimate character. (The railroad was already here when the town was founded, which meant that the first town fathers didn't have to plan extra width on main street for long wagon teams and mule trains to swing around.)

A classic western ski town has to have a classic locals' bar. Crested Butte has two. The Wooden Nickel is the hangout of choice for ski area types, patrollers and instructors. Whereas the down-valley locals prefer Kochevars (pronounced Ka-chivers) for serious drinking and pool playing; it's still owned by the Kochevar family that built it in 1900, which makes it the oldest bar in town.

Crested Butte is full of restaurants with great atmosphere; but unfortunately shy on restaurants with great cuisine. After some hesitation and a lot of testing, I've concluded that the best restaurant in town is Soupçon, a miniature historic log cabin in a back alley where you're likely to enjoy some very imaginative and refined cooking. Runner-up is Le Bosquet which is far more conventional. *The* place for hearty breakfasts is the Forest Queen. And my favorite morning rendezvous for fresh coffee, fresher pastries and the Denver paper is a delightful cafe/bakery, appropriately called the Bakery Cafe.

Lodging in old Crested Butte is scarce compared to the wide gamut up at Mt. Crested Butte, only a couple of hundred pillows at most. But the insider's best bet is the Elk Mountain Lodge, once an in-town boarding house for miners. The Elk Mountain Lodge was formerly owned by the town's biggest employer, CF&I (Colorado Fuel and Iron), and today has been totally refurbished into a delightful inn.

CRESTED BUTTE DATA

KEY PHONE NUMBER

For   Snow Conditions
       Ski Area Information
       & Central Reservations   1-800-544-8448

TRANSPORTATION

By car, 30 minute drive from Gunnison on highway 135.
By limo, from Gunnison/Crested Butte Airport
By plane, via American, United, Delta, Continental and Mesa to Gunnison/Crested Butte Airport.

MOUNTAIN STATISTICS

Vertical Drop	2,300 feet
Summit Elev.	11,400 feet
Bottom Elev.	9,100 feet
Skiing Terrain	877 acres
Number of Lifts	11 including 2 surface lifts
Longest Run	1.9 miles
Uphill Capacity	13,550 per hour
Snowboarding	Yes

A lot of skiers have seen young telemarkers, flashing by in their curious but elegant kneeling position. And a lot of downhill skiers have tried cross-country skiing in a track, may even own their own cross country gear. But even most cross-country enthusiasts have never tried telemark turns themselves. Telemarking well in all conditions is a real challenge, but just learning the turn is easy. If you have a pair of cross-country skis (you don't need special tele skis to learn the basics) and want to try, do it like this.

First get used to the telemark stance in a straight run down a very gentle slope. Slide your skis apart, fore and aft, as you drop into a semi-keeling position: the rear knee almost touching the ski, the front knee bent at 90°. Then rise and slide the rear ski forward as you drop into the opposite telemark position, front and back legs reversed. And repeat a couple of times.

Now do a couple of fast smooth wedge turns with your feet pretty close together (i.e. a small, narrow wedge). Then, halfway through one of these wedge turns, drop into the telemark position you've practiced earlier, outside ski ahead, inside ski trailing. (That is, if you're turning right, you'll slide your left ski ahead, and let your right ski drop back as you kneel.) This wedge-telemark works just like a stem christy to get you into a beautiful sliding finish, only this time it's a telemark finish to your turn rather than a christy skid. Believe me, it's easy...if you try it from a narrow wedge.

Next a few more of these wedge telemarks – fairly long turns – letting your skis come around on their own in the telemark position rather than forcing them quickly around. Progressively narrow your wedge more and more, while skiing somewhat faster, and in about 15 minutes you'll be guiding a pure telemark turn down you gentle practice hill. A packed beginner slope at a downhill ski area is the ideal spot for this eye-opening experiment.

CHAPTER 14   TELLURIDE

It's true confession time. I may as well tell you up-front, because it will be evident anyway, that Telluride is my personal favorite. Not, I hasten to add, because it has anything like the best skiing, much less the slickest amenities, or liveliest resort atmosphere – but simply because the Telluride valley is the most beautiful mountain hideaway I've found yet, in the Rockies, or in any other range for that matter. This steep-sided box canyon is a mind-boggling setting for a lovely small-to-medium sized ski area that nonetheless reserves some fierce challenges for expert skiers. At the end of the canyon nestles a tiny town that's still working on a graceful transition from funky hardrock mining community to a polished resort. Telluride is my adopted home; I moved here in 1976 when the local mine still employed 300 miners. The tunnels are shut now, the mill padlocked, and skiers, tourists and tee-shirt merchants in nearly equal numbers have discovered this enchanted valley. Telluride has changed dramatically, is still changing, and I'm still in love with the place.

Why? Maybe the thirteen and fourteen-thousand foot peaks of these San Juan mountains, ringing the valley and the ski area, or the waterfalls that turn into giant crystal organ pipes in winter, or the sunsets that slant through this east-west canyon like flash floods of liquid gold, or the cockeyed Victorian houses self-consciously spiffy in their new paint. Telluride is outrageously beautiful every day of the year, even more so in winter.

The ski area suffers from the same sort of bad rep as Taos. From town it looks radically steep – it is – and actually most of the "reasonable" or everyday skiing for real people is on the other side of the mountain, facing west with a hundred-mile view all the way to the Utah border. Two runs down the front face, the *Plunge* and the *Spiral Stairs*, are indeed the longest, steepest bump runs in America. But just as with

Taos, there are plenty of alternatives for every level of skier.

THE SHAPE AND LAYOUT OF THE MOUNTAIN

Telluride is a two-sided ski mountain with two bases. The front face rising dramatically above town has two separate lift access routes. The Coonskin chair at the entrance to town rises up to a mid point on the long ridge-like crest of the mountain; and the Oak Street lift from the center of town and its continuation, the Plunge triple chair, take skiers over 3,000 vertical feet up to the very top. All the skiing on this side is serious except for one zig-zag road, the *Telluride Trail* that provides a comfortable come-home route for weaker skiers who are too self conscious to ride the Coonskin lift back down into town. The rest of the runs on the front are marked blue and black, but skiers should beware: a blue run on Telluride's face would be black at most areas, a black run would be double black elsewhere.

The backside – which is really the *main side*, because that's where most of the skiing is – is large and spread out and far, far friendlier for mere mortals. I've called Telluride a medium-small ski area, but it is spread out in separate pods over an amazingly large but diffuse mountain. The skiing zones are fragmented into these separate pods by a host of natural obstacles: cliff bands, creek beds and secondary hill-like summits. When you actually total up the amount of skiing available, it's less than one would expect. Curiously this doesn't matter very much, because Telluride's mountain capacity is still much bigger than its bed base. In the 16 years since the ski area first opened, no one here has ever seen a real lift line. Which means you can get in as much skiing as your legs can take. There are seven lifts on the back or "friendly" side of the mountain (including a poma on the race hill). We'll look at them in more detail as I recommend runs for different level skiers.

There is also a second base to the ski area on this "other" side. Not just a base lodge, but a second village in the making. A short drive around the mountain from town, the ski corporation is constructing a brand new resort, The Mountain Village at Telluride – a handsome project with lots of elegant stonework, southwestern inspired tile roofs and most of all, a genuinely spectacular setting in a wide meadow at the foot of lifts 3 and 4, the main intermediate skiing zone. But such projects take years, and today this area is more a village-to-be than a completed village. There is already one hip luncheon restaurant in the Mountain Village, the Cactus Cafe; and a bus shuttle connects it with town for beginners, who aren't ready to ski from one side of the mountain to the other, or for non skiers.

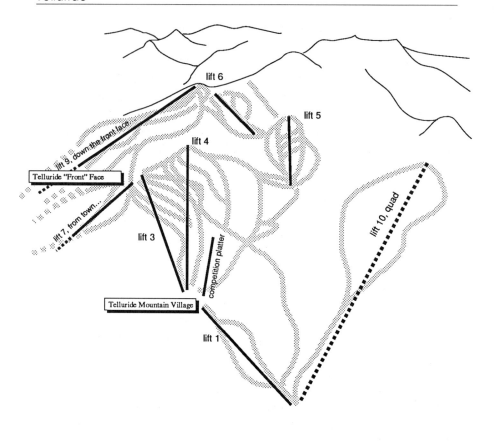

Telluride—
a sketch map of the "back" which is also the "main" side of the ski mountain.
For details consult a current area trail map.

TELLURIDE FOR AVERAGE SKIERS

From town, most skiers will want to take the Coonskin lift and immediately head down the other side, at least for a warm up run or two. If, instead, you decide to take lifts 8 and 9, the Oak Street and Plunge lifts, to the very top, you will find that there is only one comfortable non-black run off the top, *See Forever*, a long ridge-line cruiser that doesn't have quite as good a view as the name suggests because it is lined with dense forest for most of its length. *See Forever* takes you back down to the top of the Coonskin lift anyway, so it's faster to begin your day down there, and only head up to the top of the mountain around noon to enjoy lunch with a view – the most spectacular view from any Colorado ski area – at the tiny Plunge cafe.

At the top of Coonskin you are standing on the rim of a large forested bowl that contains Telluride's greatest concentration of intermediate trails. The runs to your left are easier (and *Village Bypass* is the absolute easiest way down this side of the mountain, two runs straight ahead of you, *Hermit* and *Smuggler*, are rather steep and occasionally lightly moguled; to the right, the runs stretch out, longer and smoother, wide boulevards with sustained pitch but no sudden drops. *Butterfly* drops straight down to the big mid-mountain restaurant at Gorono Park, and *Lower See Forever*, bears right all the way down to the lift. Or should I say lifts?

You run out of hill at the edge of the Mountain Village and coast up to lifts 3 and 4, a double and a triple, that together serve over 50% of the good intermediate skiing on the mountain. Chair 3 takes you back to the ridge by the Coonskin lift terminal, chair 4 is longer and opens up more additional runs. The least skied run off chair 4 is *Humbolt Draw*, a lovely half-hidden valley, twisting like an outsize toboggan run, that's well worth checking out.

From the top of 4 you can also traverse around the corner on a road to lift 5, which once again feels like a separate little ski area. It's an important one though, because it features the only consistently easy, friendly bump run at Telluride, *Palmyra*. If you have ambitions to ski the *Plunge* or other hard black runs, polishing your bump turns on *Palmyra* first is a very good idea. And from the top of 5 you can also traverse down and right to lift 6, which takes you up to the top of the ski mountain.

As I mentioned before this is a zero option take-off point for intermediate (blue run only) skiers, since *See Forever* is the only non-threatening, non-moguled run off the top. But halfway down *See Forever*, you'll see another interesting alternative, *Lookout*. *Lookout* dives off the ridge and down the front face, and it is certainly the most reasonable run on the front face for average skiers. Plunging views of town like a miniature doll-house community beneath your skis provide some of the visual drama of harder front face runs with none of the potential trauma. *Lookout* is wide, usually well groomed and not the slightest bit threatening. In this it's quite different from *Coonskin* or *Woozleys*, two other runs down the front that are marked blue but are *bad*, in the good sense of course. And that's it folks. Honest intermediates won't want to hang out much on lift 10, about which I'll tell you more in a minute.

TELLURIDE FOR BEGINNERS AND NOVICES

Beginners here have it made. Lift 1 is a wide and gracious practice universe for first-timers and emerging novices. It serves the *Meadows*, rolling slightly inclined flats just below the Mountain Village. The only inconvenience for first-timers is the bus ride around from town, but believe me there is no learning terrain for never-evers on the Telluride side of the mountain. Security and rapid progress is worth a twenty minute bus ride through great scenery.

Almost as soon as they've mastered a solid wedge, and certainly with some kind of sloppy basic christy, novice skiers can take the Coonskin lift up from town and still make it safely down to the beginner area by following *Village Bypass* all the way left and down. Almost more of a ski tour than a run, this trail brings one down to the *Meadows*, avoiding all traffic, all steeps, even mini-steeps, through a lovely aspen forest.

Finally there's lift 10, slanting up into thick forest from the base lodge at the bottom of chair 1. As your christies begin to improve, you'll find the two long runs on chair 10 very suitable, almost ideal. Ideal for the sort of mileage that makes progress inevitable. But I want to add that for better skiers, chair 10 is one of the most pointless pieces of lift engineering ever dreamed up. Yes, it is a state-of-the-art, high speed detachable quad. But you'll understand the problem when you learn that Telluride locals have nicknamed it "the lift to nowhere." In actual fact, it's more a real-estate lift than a ski lift, designed to provide ski-in, ski-out access to high-ticket homesites adjoining the Mountain Village. This is not what I mean by the white revolution. Stronger skiers should certainly venture over to lift 10 anyway, just to see what's what, but you won't spend much time there.

TELLURIDE FOR EXPERTS

Despite all its intermediate skiing, Telluride has been stereotyped in the folklore of Colorado skiing as an experts' mountain. Fair or unfair? A bit of both. The bell shaped curve operates here too, and you'll find more intermediates enjoying themselves on any given day at Telluride than experts. But it's also true that the better you are, the better you'll like this mountain. To ski every run well at Telluride demands much more skill than it does at Steamboat or Snowmass. But if this is, in some sense, an experts' mountain, it's also a mountain for a particular breed of expert skier. Telluride is bumper heaven.

Telluride's black slopes are very steep, always bumped out. And these bumps are really wild. It's not that they're badly formed; they're

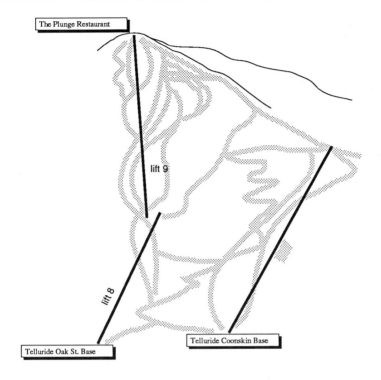

The Front Face at Telluride—
a sketch map showing the main runs and lifts, the Telluride Trail, the only easy way down this side,
is the zig-zag path leading down to the Coonskin base from the top of lift 7.
Check the area trail map for details.

simply big, awesomely big, and deep. To use the appropriate bump
skiers' vernacular, Telluride's bumps are "gnarly."

There are two main mogul skiing zones at Telluride. The first, short
and sweet, is lift 6 sometimes just called Apex, after *Apex Glade*, the
large half-open area to the north of the lift. The skiing here is just as
"interesting" as on the front face, but the runs are much, much shorter.
Zulu Queen, a narrow slot through the woods, is the hardest line, *Silver
Glade* and *Apex Glade* are the most fun, and *Allais Alley*, under the lift
strictly for showoffs. Even the forest between the runs on six is moguled! The second, legendary bump zone comprises the long black runs
coming right off the top and tumbling down the front in a 2,500 vertical
foot non-stop cascade. The best shaped moguls on the front are found
on *Mammoth Slide*, the worst on *Kant-Mak-M*, but both these runs eventually feed into the middle of the *Stairs*. For years known as the *Spiral*

Stairs, this great run has now been split in two on the map – one side called *Spiral*, the other *Stairs*. No matter, the *Stairs* is the grandaddy of mean mogul runs. It starts innocently enough, branching off from *See Forever* ridge at *Joint Point*. A quarter mile later it simply drops out from under you. The start is breathtaking; and the rest – once you recover from the sudden visual impact of coming over a lip and looking straight down almost three thousand feet – is just as hard. I rank the *Stairs*, along with the top pitch of *Mont Fort* at Verbier and the *West Face* of KT22 at Squaw, among the steepest hardest bump runs anywhere. Don't ski it your first morning in Telluride. Just left of the *Stairs* is the *Plunge*, which is a run of a different color, so to speak. It's still black – or should be, even though the ski area inexplicably colored it blue on last year's trail map, which got a lot of innocent skiers into trouble – but it's far, far easier than the *Stairs*. And just as famous.

Telluride's final treat for expert skiers is *Gold Hill*. This is an area of steep chutes *above* the top of the ski area that are now controlled and, as often as possible, opened by the patrol. Skiers hike uphill for ten to twenty minutes to reach lines like *Killer*, *Electra* and *Little Rose*, several hundred vertical feet of mixed snow and cut-up powder, bottoming out in a long traverse back to lift 5. All the thrill of out-of-bounds skiing, only it's legal and the snow is safe, when the patrol opens the gate. But although the *Gold Hill* "powder preserve" is marked double black on the trial map, it isn't nearly as serious as the big bump runs on the face that are mere black diamonds.

A TINY TOWN AND ITS TREASURES

Telluride (including its box canyon) is only a little more than four blocks wide. It's a miniature mining town, not another Aspen, rough natured and warm-hearted. Where volunteer fire fighters coexist uneasily with Lear Jets parking at the new airport outside town. Cars are unnecessary, and if you need to go clear to the other end of town, say with a bag of groceries over one shoulder and skis on the other, you can always take the free town bus. And just what do you do in Telluride when you're not standing around with a crick in your neck admiring the peaks?

Leimgruber's, near the Coonskin base, is a popular post-Plunge pub with its vast collection of imported German beers. And downtown, the Sheridan Bar is a good example of turn-of-the-century mining town chic. But reallyTelluride is still too small and too down-home to compete in big-league apres-ski, although there are always a couple of bar/clubs with live music. If any sort of show is playing in the old Sheridan Opera

House – movie, amateur theatrical or concert – don't miss it. The Sheridan is one of the most beautiful gold-rush opera houses left in Colorado. And for the last word in anti-slickness, you can rent a pair of skates and walk over to the town park to skate on an outdoor oval under the giant cliffs of Bear Creek.

Eating out is easy. Telluride has better restaurants than one would guess, or perhaps than it deserves. The two finest are the Silver Glade, where fresh fish is flown in daily and the mesquite grill is more than just a trendy accessory; and La Marmotte, a French restaurant that fits beautifully into a historic brick "ice house," two blocks below main street. Friends of mine from Vail and Aspen who eat regularly at La Marmotte every time they visit, come back raving: "We don't have anything this good back home..." which is a kind of ultimate food review in a Colorado ski resort. At the other end of the spectrum, Telluride is blessed with two bakeries. Baked in Telluride, located in an old tin-sided warehouse, produces the best bagels this side of Katz' delicatessen; and Gregor's on main street is fresh-bread heaven for anyone who appreciate classical European style baking.

All the normal ski area lodging options are found here too, plus a couple of gems. The New Sheridan Hotel (which was already called the "New Sheridan" when William Jennings Bryan gave his celebrated "cross of gold" speech in front of it) is Telluride's equivalent of the Ritz and boasts the only elevator in San Miguel County! In recent years, we've seen the beginning of a trend toward intimate Bed & Breakfast Inns rather than simply building more and more condo blocks. (The fanciest of these Bed and Breakfasts is the San Sophia.) And finally, if you want to break the usual vacation mold, you should consider staying at Skyline Ranch, an incredibly beautiful and romantic old-time guest ranch just a few miles outside town.

TELLURIDE DATA

Snow Conditions	(303) 728-3614
Ski Area Information	(303)728-4424
Central Reservations	800-525-3455
also	(303) 728-4431

TRANSPORTATION

By car, 1 1/2 hour drive south from Montrose or 1 hour 45 minutes north from Cortez.
By van from Telluride or Montrose airports.
By plane, via Continental Express and Mesa Airlines to Telluride Airport.

MOUNTAIN STATISTICS

Vertical Drop	3,155 feet
Summit Elev.	11,890 feet
Base Elevation	8,735 feet
Skiing Terrain	735 acres
Longest Run	2.85 miles
Number of Lifts	10 including one high speed detachable quad and 1 surface lift.
Uphill Capacity	10,836 skiers per hour
Snowboarding	Yes

SKI TECH: SKIING SUPER BUMPS

Skiing bumps is one thing, skiing extra big, extra steep bumps quite another. As usual there are a few tricks to it. And, like an advanced graduate course at the university, there are prerequisites. Unless you can ski medium and small bumps smoothly and efficiently, you'll be floundering on serious bump runs like the Spiral Stairs at Telluride. But given the basics, here's how to adapt them to tougher stuff.

Balance, quickness and poles. On mega-bumps the slope changes so radically from one moment to the next that you're always playing catch up with your skis, which tend to drop out form under you in the steep gullies. The solution is faster, more dynamic pole action. By the time your skis have pivoted into the fall line, you should already be reaching straight down the hill with your pole for the next bump. In effect, this pulls your body forward so you can keep up with your skis and, of course, gets you ready for the next turn.

But often in big hard bumps there isn't much room to finish your turn between one bump and the next, so once again speed control becomes an issue. The solution is simply to accept a little more speed and then, periodically, wherever there's room to do so, complete your turn by curving up and over the shoulder of the next bump. This extra uphill hook will cut your speed way back from time to time.

As you ski faster, in bigger bumps, you will often feel yourself compressed, your legs pushed up beneath you, by the force with which you contact the bump. This compression is a natural form of shock absorbing, but it only works once. To use your legs as shock absorbers again, on the next bump, you need to make a continual effort to extend your feet and legs back down into the trough as you come over the lip of the bump, stretching out to fill up the available space, getting tall to absorb the next compression.

Of course, that's not the whole story of super bumps, but it's a good start. You'll find more information, more detail, more help with this and other skiing challenges in my book, Breakthrough on Skis, a Vintage paperback from Random House.

CHAPTER 15 PURGATORY

Purgatory fits perfectly into my category of ski areas in Colorado's soulful southwest: small, remote and charming. Its charm however is a fragmented one. Purgatory is located in the southern San Juan mountains – not far from Telluride in a straight line on the map, but a helluva long way around by road – with grandiose views of granite peaks and deep gorges. But despite some ambitious base development in recent years, the town that naturally "goes with" Purgatory – Durango – isn't at the foot of the slopes, as it certainly would be if this were really the best of all possible worlds. Instead, Durango lies half an hour's drive to the south, where the Animas River flows out of the mountains into the first high red mesas of Anasazi country. If fate had only put these two together....

Durango is a great western town, more a small city than a town actually, with an old historic main street, a state college, and enough good shops, restaurants and lodging to make most ski towns jealous. But you don't get to walk home at night watching the moonlight painting milky brushstrokes down runs you've schussed the same afternoon. Pity.

The Purgatory-Durango combination still works, and it's been a long-time favorite with skiers from Albuquerque, Phoenix and the southwest. The ski experience at Purgatory is intimate and low-key rather than challenging and grand, but the skier service level is high, and the natives friendly. It's hard not to like Purgatory.

HOW THE MOUNTAIN WORKS

The mountain you see when you arrive at the base faces due east, across the great hollowed out gorge of the Animas river, with a stunning view of a rugged sub-range, appropriately called the Twilight Peaks, on the other side of the canyon. Lifts 6 and 1 march right up the front face which looks, and is, respectably steep; while lift 4 slants off to the right, opening up an area of friendly green runs, where novices will spend most of their time. (Purgatory's chairs, by the way, are numbered in the order in which they were built.) The best time of day for the front face is early and mid morning to take advantage of the direct early light; by late afternoon you're liable to find crusty or scraped conditions there.

As soon as you tire of the front side, you'll discover that the mountain folds or wraps around the corner to the right, into a side valley. And the runs on this "side mountain" (served by lifts 2, 3, 5 and 8) face almost due north. That makes for a pretty fair trade off: either great views (on the front) or great snow (on the side). Most of the skiing is found on this "side mountain," which is quite a bit bigger than the front. So during the course of a day at Purgatory you'll wind up traversing the mountain from one side to the other a couple of times. It helps to know that the runs marked *Parkway* or *Expressway* are the best cross-mountain trails.

I should tell you too that, like Copper Mountain, Purgatory is wider than it is tall. Most of the area is what you could call "one-lift high," a tad less than 2,000 vertical feet; but it stretches so far around to the side that one has the impression of skiing on a big and complex mountain. It is certainly a much bigger place than what you see from the road

The large "side mountain" is naturally zoned or divided into skiing terrain for different abilities. It starts out quite easy with a lot of green runs and easy blues on lift 2. (Many locals consider lift 2 to be part of the "front" since the other chairs are much further around the corner.) Then, the farther across you go, the harder and more stimulating the skiing is. Chairs 3 and 5 serve the middle area of this "side mountain," a zone of longer blue runs with a couple of friendly blacks. Chair 5 is notable also because it brings you to a smashing mountain restaurant, Dante's Den, upstairs in the mid-mountain warming hut/cafeteria building. The food at this sit-down restaurant is head and shoulders above the fare at "fancy" mountain restaurants at most Colorado ski mountains.

And finally, if you cross all the way over, skiing down an uninspired, expressway of a run called *Legends*, you'll arrive at the last and newest chair, number 8. Lift 8 serves the steepest skiing on the north side, an entire zone also called *The Legends*. Here there are a number of black runs, and an exceptional area near the top where *Blackburn's Bash* and *Paul's Park* wander through steep open forest glades – a nice contrast with the clearly defined trails on the rest of the mountain. The two most exciting runs at *The Legends* are *Ray's Ridge*

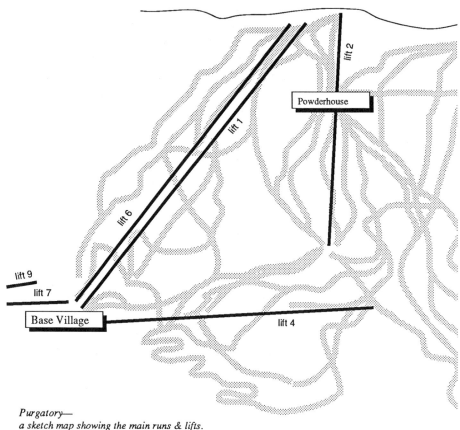

Purgatory—
a sketch map showing the main runs & lifts.
For greater detail, consult a current ski area trail map.
(Note: the maps on these two pages overlap in the center.)

and *Elliot's*: steep, varied terrain with attractive banked sides to play on.

Purgatory runs, gentle or tough, share a common flavor, a special character which makes skiing here intriguing but not effortless. Purgatory is a roller coaster, where the pitch of the slope is seldom continuous. There are numerous breakaways in almost every trail, a roller-coaster sequence of steeps and flats with abrupt sometimes exciting transitions. These transitions aren't so abrupt that they'll get you into trouble, but they do keep you on your toes, then heels, then toes, etc…. Personally I love this sort of skiing, where you are constantly forced to adapt and adjust to changing terrain – skiing a real and variable mountain shape

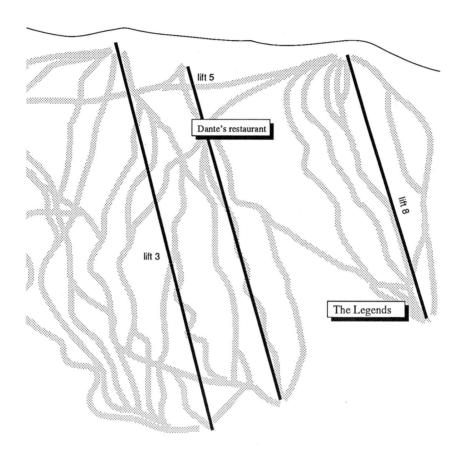

lift 5

Dante's restaurant

lift 8

lift 3

The Legends

rather than slopes of man-made smoothness. But you have to be careful
not to blind jump any of these sudden lips where the slope changes
angle; or conversely, not to stop beneath any of these breaks in pitch
where a flying teenager might nail you.

I'm less enthused about the other characteristic of Purgatory trails.
I find them all a bit narrow for my taste – the one exception being *Dead
Spike*, right in the middle of the northern side of the mountain. Everything else being equal, skiers, even expert skiers, always ski better and
feel freer on wider runs. If most of the runs at Purgatory could be
widened 50%, they'd have a magical mountain here.

DRINKING, DINING AND DANCING IN DURANGO

Despite some really good looking development at the base of the ski mountain, including a pedestrian plaza that has a great feel to it and great view too, there just isn't much to do up there except ski. Most Purgatory skiers will still head for Durango after the last run.

Durango is an easy town to find one's way around in, since it's organized around a traditional Western main-street axis. The south end of Main Street is the old section of town with the last two or three blocks really qualifying as a historic core. One of the most imposing buildings on lower Main Street is also the best place in town to stay, the elegant, historic Strater Hotel. This grand four-story red brick building is both a treat and a bargain. In Aspen its rooms with their all antique furnishings would go for three of four times the price. It also houses two other Durango musts: The Diamond Belle Saloon, an old time bar that's still a marvel despite bartenders in corny period costumes; and the Diamond Circle Theatre, a classic melodrama and vaudeville stage where the corny old-time costumes are, in fact, just right.

The best food in Durango, however, is not in the Strater but a few blocks away at an Italian restaurant called Ariano's. This is a real find, unpretentious and modestly priced, where they make their own pasta daily and serve dishes that would do credit to Vanessi's in San Francisco. Across the street from Ariano's, you can two-step at the Sundance Saloon, the local honky tonk and western dance parlor, where there's always a live country and western band on stage. Unfortunately the one down-home, out-west, long-time Durango tradition that winter ski guests can't enjoy is the weekly rodeo at the fairgrounds, which is a summer only happening. Colorado summer, of course, is another story, another book, another adventure.

PURGATORY DATA

Ski Area Information	800-525-0892
	303-247-9000(in Colorado)
Central Reservations	800-247-9000
	(303) 247-8900 (in Colorado)

TRANSPORTATION

By car, 30 minute drive from Durango north on U.S. Highway 550.

By plane, via America West, United Express, Continental Express, or Southwest Airlines to the Durango-La Plata County Airport, 44 miles south of Purgatory.

MOUNTAIN STATISTICS

Vertical Drop	2,029 feet
Summit Elev.	10,822 feet
Base Elevation	8,793 feet
Skiing Terrain	630 acres
Number of Lifts	9
Longest Run	2 miles
Uphill Capacity	12,700
Snowboarding	Yes

Here we are, at the end of another book. For me, the end of another wonderful winter, skiing all over Colorado. For you, I hope, just the beginning of many new adventures on Colorado's ski slopes....

But nothing ends quite so neatly. Just as no two snowflakes are ever the same, neither are any two ski seasons. The white revolution in ski area services won't stop in 1989, or 1990, or.... Nor in fact does this white revolution stop at Colorado's borders. Every few seasons, it seems, there may be a brand-new world out there for us skiers.

Already this guide has been extensively revised since it's sell-out first edition, reflecting new lifts, new runs, new realities on Colorado slopes. And this book is only the first in our on-going series of skier's guides.

If you found this volume useful, you'll want to check out *The Insider's Guides to the Best Skiing in Utah*, by Peter Shelton, which is already available. And other guides to the best skiing in New England, California (and the West Coast) and the Alps, will be ready soon.

The continual revision and improvement of our ski-guide series will be made a lot easier by the flexible Macintosh computer-based publishing system we're using. But it will also be made easier by your feedback, suggestions, comments, and wishes. What did you like about this book? What worked for you and what didn't? What would you like to see in future editions? Should we make an effort to include more illustrations? More maps? More ski tips? And what sort?

You get the idea – but to make sure that we get your ideas, you can write to:

> Western Eye Press / Ski Guides
> Box 917
> Telluride, Colorado 81435

Thanks, and good skiing!
Lito Tejada-Flores